Christian Conversion in Context

Christian Conversion in Context

Hans Kasdorf

Foreword by Arthur F. Glasser

HERALD PRESS
Scottdale, Pennsylvania
Kitchener, Ontario
1980

Library of Congress Cataloging in Publication Data

Kasdorf, Hans.
    Christian conversion in context.

    Bibliography: p.
    Includes index.
    1. Conversion. I. Title.
    BV4916.K28   248.2'4   80-12871
    ISBN 0-8361-1926-6 (pbk.)

CHRISTIAN CONVERSION IN CONTEXT
Copyright © 1980 by Herald Press, Scottdale, PA 15683
    Published simultaneously in Canada by Herald Press,
    Kitchener, Ont. N2G 4M5
Library of Congress Catalog Card Number: 80-12871
International Standard Book Number: 0-8361-1926-6
Printed in the United States of America
Design by Alice B. Shetler/Cover Photo by David Hiebert

15 14 13 12 11 10 9 8 7 6 5 4 3 2 1

To Frieda and our children—
Dianne and Michael, David and Evelyn,
who share in the converted
life under the lordship of Christ—
I dedicate this book.

Contents

List of Figures

Foreword

How-to-do-it books crowd best-seller lists in the religious market these days offering ready advice on how to be born again or how to give away your faith. They imply that man the manipulator is somehow able at will to bring about profound spiritual change in the inner world of his heart and transform the lives of others through the application of carefully devised formulas. Good results are guaranteed! God cannot but respond and make people whole and happy!

But *Christian Conversion in Context* speaks differently. God is central. His grace identifies him as the Seeker, and a soiled, estranged humanity as the object of His gracious seeking. His voice in Scripture is reverently heard. This means that in humility the word "mystery" must be written large over all that He is and does. But it also means that one can have confidence in His self-disclosure in the gospel. Nonetheless, the author does not minimize human responsibility. He delineates conversion as the fundamental decision of an individual in response to God's call to repentance and faith. It embraces the need for repudiating oneself, a self-dethronement that must precede the deliberate enthronement of Jesus Christ as Lord of heart and life.

What makes this exploration so refreshingly different is not only its faithful handling of biblical concepts related to human sinfulness, but also its careful treatment of the nature of conversion and the relation between church and convert. Dr. Kasdorf skillfully incorporates the insights of anthropologically informed missiologists into our understanding of the ways of God in His redemptive search for His people. Thus this is an ethnotheological, as well as an exegetical, study. The author also examines a variety of religious experiences, ranging from the sixteenth-century Anabaptist discoveries of life and holiness in Christ to contemporary incidents drawn from his own missionary experience in Latin America. These add authenticity to the book and give amplification to Kasdorf's thesis.

Those who ponder *Christian Conversion in Context* will be renewed in their conviction that God is at work in the world today. They will sense in a new way that those who choose to work with Him gain fresh awareness of the continued relevance of Scripture and the complete sufficiency of Christ in meeting men and women in their spiritual need.

Arthur F. Glasser, Dean
School of World Mission
Fuller Theological Seminary
Pasadena, California

Author's Preface

In addition to personal reading and reflection on the topic of conversion from a variety of perspectives, I have had many occasions in evangelistic, missionary, and church ministries to witness personally the Holy Spirit's power in the transformation of people's lives, resulting in new value systems and lifestyles. Attending lectures and seminars on conversion as well as discussing the subject with teachers, students, and colleagues of various schools has sharpened my understanding and added insight. The book is an outgrowth of the practical and the academic.

When I wrote the first draft several years ago, my objective was solely to define and clarify for myself the issues involved in the complexity of processes of Christian conversion. Only after several of my colleagues at Fresno Pacific College and the Mennonite Brethren Biblical Seminary read the manuscript and responded with constructive criticism did the thought of sharing the material with other Christian workers begin to emerge. In subsequent revisions, I eliminated technical points, explained those considered appropriate as vehicles of thought, expanded where necessary, improved the diagrams, and supplemented the majority of chapters with a case story. I hope the book will help clarify conversion and lead readers to a greater commitment to present the gospel to those in spiritual need.

I wish to express my gratitude to Charles H. Kraft of the School of World Mission, Fuller Theological Seminary, who has been the single most thought-provoking person in my life on the present subject, and has challenged me to wrestle with the issue of conversion; to my colleagues, Delbert Wiens of Fresno Pacific College, to D. Edmund Hiebert, Elmer Martens, and Henry Schmidt of the Biblical Seminary for their criticisms and encouragement, and to Thomas and Elizabeth Brewster, visiting professors at the Church Mission Institute in Fresno, for reading and making valuable suggestions to improve the present manuscript; to my students of the Theological Workers Course at the Instituto Biblico Asunción for challenging some of my assumptions; to my daughter Dianne and her husband, Michael, for giving a professional touch to the diagrams; and to my wife for typing the manuscript and assisting in countless ways.

The objective of this book is to stimulate students and teachers, pastors and missionaries, as well as other Christian men and women from all walks of life—particularly those dedicated to cross-cultural communication of the gospel—to see that Christian conversion does not follow a stereotyped pattern but may take a variety of forms both personal and multipersonal. The Holy Spirit is unbound in His ways and means to convert people and help them become responsible members of the believers' church which exists to serve and glorify God between the resurrection and coming again of Jesus Christ, the Lord.

Hans Kasdorf
Fresno, California

PART I
Introduction

Chapter 1

Introducing the Subject

God's program in the world is to make saints out of sinners.
—*Myron S. Augsburger, 1961*

An impressive list of recent publications, books, essays in academic journals, and shorter articles in religious magazines and church papers on conversion demonstrates indisputably the revived interest in the subject.° In fact, Christian conversion in recent years has occupied the thinking of theologians and church statesmen, psychologists and social anthropologists, missionaries and evangelists, philosophers and historians, clergy and laity alike. The approaches have varied, depending on the academic and professional orientation or on the theological and religious persuasion of the respective writers.

Even in countries like the Soviet Union Christian conversion is no foreign concept. Thus the Orthodox author Lewitin-Krassnow wrote early in 1968 in a letter to Pope

---

°A separate "Bibliography on Conversion" of over 200 items has been compiled by the author and is available by writing to him in Fresno.

Paul VI about the religious revival among Russian youth. Speaking about cases of conversion to Christianity within his own church, Lewitin-Krassnow asserted that the Baptists could "pride themselves of even larger numbers of conversions. However all conversions take place within the ranks of the unbelieving youth," not infrequently "the sons of Moscow communists" among them. "As one observes the dynamic and intensity of the religious revival of these young people," attests Lewitin-Krassnow, "it is not exaggerated to say that their fervor and enthusiasm is not behind that of the early Christians." In view of their genuineness on the one hand, and the intense conflicts emerging as a result of the conversion on the other, continues the Russian author, "one is inevitably reminded of the words in the Gospel of John 3:8, 'The wind blows where it wills, and you hear the sound of it, but you do not know whence it comes or whither it goes; so it is with every one who is born of the Spirit' " (Scheffbuch, 1973:6, translation mine).

Case Story: The Conversion of a Sorcerer

Mr. Wei had once been a notorious sorcerer. He belonged to a former headhunting tribe of Taiwan. Whenever a head had been taken, his people would gather for a tribal dance lasting all night. It was Mr. Wei's job to drive the demons out of the skull, and then put it at the sacred place with many other skulls.

One day in September 1968, Taiwan missionaries, Lowell and Naomi Williamson of the Oriental Missionary Society (OMS), along with a tribal pastor, called on Wei and his family. After relating his evil dreams, involvement with demon worship, sorcery, and headhunting, the dialogue between Wei and the missionaries tells his conversion experience (Williamson, 1969:3-5).

Mr. Wei, tell us how you were converted.

My son (father of Miss Wei Be Ling, a student in the OMS seminary) was converted several years earlier. He was led to the Lord by Mr. Wu, a fellow worker at the Railway Hospital. Mr. Wu was and is a pastor of the OMS Ren Li Church. My son often talked to me about Christ.

Did you accept Christ then?

No, not till several years later, although Mr. Wu and Peter Lin (called "The Fisherman" because of hundreds he has won to Christ) often witnessed to me. I just couldn't free myself from the demons. Then one night before a tribal dance, I dreamed that I was standing on the road and an American missionary approached me, putting a brand on my forehead. The next day I went to the dance, but could not forget the dream. So I went home and did not dance. For a whole week, I was violently ill. Many at the Ren Li Church were praying for me. . . . Mr. Wu and Mr. Lin visited me again, and that day I accepted Christ as my Savior. . . .

Have you been bothered with demons since your conversion?

For about two years following my conversion, I occasionally had those dreams, but the demons never entered the house; they always stayed outside. Two years later, however, the church people came and we had a worship service here in the house. Since then, I have had no evil dreams.

How has your conversion affected you physically?

It is a great relief to be free from demons. I have not been sick once since my conversion ten years ago. I now sleep soundly.

Setting the Stage

The present study is divided into four parts, of which the first is designed to introduce frequently occurring concepts and to clarify their meaning. Part Two deals with conversion as understood in the context of Scripture—both the Old and the New Testaments. It is significant to bear in mind that conversion today—as always—is made imperative by humanity's ever-besetting problem—the problem of sin. Sin is the underlying cause which separtes and estranges persons from their Maker; the conversion experience is the healing factor that unites and reconciles individuals with their Maker. Therefore, the objective of the second section is to deal with the essence of conversion as seen in the biblical context of sin and salvation. Ever since the Fall, God is always the Seeker; man is always the object sought.

Part Three attempts to delineate the conversion experience within the matrix of various concerns. The purpose there is to express and to clarify the "ethnotheologian's" approach to Christian conversion, that major experience of life transformation, brought about by the Spirit of God in a variety of different settings. More specifically, the emphasis there is on the psychological, theological, missiological, generational, and ethnological understanding of conversion. The investigation there focuses less on the "why" and "what" than on the "how" of conversion.

The final part is given to the essence of the believers' church and its role and function in relationship to conversion. The focus is on the church as the body of Christ, seeking to carry out its mandate to both the unconverted in the world and the young convert within its own fold. A reciprocal relationship exists between older and newer members of the body of Christ under the headship of Jesus, Savior and Lord.

Thus the entire focus of this study is on Christian conversion as understood by the relatively new discipline known as "ethnotheology," a discipline that seeks to integrate the scientific studies of theology, sociocultural anthropology, history, and psychology with a biblical view of God, humankind, and culture. The objective is to understand the role of conversion from a biblical perspective within these various contexts.

Defining Concepts

In a provocative article, Klaus von Bismarck (1957:3) of Westphalia raises the question whether or not Christian vocabulary in our day is an obstacle to communication. He concludes that it is and believes that "the old curse of confusion of tongues and the scattering of mankind, who no longer understand one another ... has today become a reality within our individual language areas." To reduce possible communication barriers to a minimum, I shall explain those concepts most likely to be misunderstood.

The Meanings of Conversion

The varied usages of the English loan word "conversion" may illustrate what von Bismarck means by confusion of tongues in our time. In English-speaking, Western societies the term "conversion" has come to mean many things to different people. We should remember at the outset that conversion *per se* is no sacred term. It is used as much in secular as in religious literature. Even the advertising and promotional world uses it. In air terminals and other public buildings across the country, the United States Energy Research and Development Administration, for instance, displays in showcases the "underground conversion" of coal "to synthetic natural gas."

To the computer technologist, *conversion* may mean the change from one code or symbolic system to another; for a psychoanalyst it may mean the process by which repressed ideas or feelings are represented by bodily change, as a simulated physical illness; for the mathematician it may mean the change in the unit of expression; for the nuclear physicist it may mean the change of one nuclear fuel into another by the process of capturing neutrons; for the carpenter it may mean the remodeling of a bedroom into a den; for the financier it may mean the exchange of a bond into another form of security of equal value; for the sociologist it may mean the transformation of social status from one level to another; for a religious worker it may mean the substitution of one religion for another; for a theologian it may mean the change from one belief system to another. Thus the word conversion simply implies the process whereby change, transmutation, or transformation in condition, state, position, value or attitude takes place either in the mental, physical, emotional, material, religious, or ethical realm of experience (cf. Löffler, 1969:3).

David A. Shank, Mennonite minister among African Independent Churches, defines Christian conversion as the process in which Christ, "the Servant-Messiah," takes people *out of* the evil context of their sinful life-way and brings them *into* new relationships of righteousness in "the servant-community." Thus the *"out-of-into"* transforming experience becomes the very axis of conversion as Shank goes on to show (1976:6).

> Conversion means in terms of understanding God, a turn *from* the many gods, or *from* no god, or *from* "belief in" a distant, unknown, or inactive god *to* "the living God."
>
> In an understanding of the religious, it means turning *from* myth *to* event and history (covenant, exodus, exile-return, Jesus-event, church in conflict with the powers. . . .)
>
> It includes turning *from* the periodic shift in sacred and profane (ritual, initiation, festival) *to* holistic sacred lifestyle (charisma, forgiveness, service).
>
> In relation to time, it means turning *from* past *to* a new linear

future; and *from* the old age *to* the (christological) "new age."

In terms of spiritual power, it means turning *from* its use for primarily material orientation (fertility, success, prosperity) *to* primary ethical preoccupation on the one hand; it means turning *from* prayer as manipulation of power *to* prayer as discernment for decision and release of redemptive creativity.

To be human means turning *from* instrumentalism (i.e., people to be used) *to* personhood (i.e., unique value of person in creation, redemption, gifts, development) and turning *from* balance of powers, and equilibrium in roles, *to* mutuality (forgiveness, gifts, service, subordination).

Conversion in specific regard to community, means turning *from* ethnicity, tribalism, *to* open covenant based on Jesus' lordship (within the church) and *from* geographic and temporal parochialism (nationalisms) *to* the universal (present and coming) Kingdom. (Minor rearrangement of quotation mine.)

Within the context of this study I am using the word conversion to describe the religious and ethical processes of man's spiritual transformation in terms of his values, relationships, and attitudes to God, himself, and others within the matrix of his own culture and social structure. For it is always within the sociocultural and religious-ethical framework that humans operate and confront change. In this sense, "conversion indicates a change from one set of loyalties to another, involving critical experiences" (Heikkinen, 1966:1). Thus, we agree with Dr. Leon Salzman (1966:10) of Georgetown University when he says that "conversion is a general term for change and generally implies a drastic alteration of a former state."

Closely related to the whole conversion concept are such ecclesiastical terms as repentance and contrition, confession and faith, reconciliation and relationship which imply deep religious and ethical sensitivities, leading to the resolution and verdict to change one's lifestyle and world-view; they imply transformation of the old way of life, leading to a new way of life (cf. Eph. 4:22-24). Such terms as repentance and confession are perhaps best understood as describing the dimension of change *away from* something old and undesirable, whereas the terms faith and reconciliation describe the aspect of change *toward* something new and desirable. Commenting on "The Nature of Evangelism" as defined in the Lausanne Covenant, Clause 4, Michael Cassidy of South Africa states succinctly,

> If repentance is a change of mind leading to a change of direction (e.g., the Prodigal, Luke 15:17, 20), and if it is conceived primarily in negative terms as turning *from* sin, then faith is the positive turning *to* Christ and receiving (John 1:12) Him as Saviour and Lord (Colossians 2:6) (Padilla, 1976:75).

The question relating to initiative and model must inevitably be raised. When we think in terms of *Heilsgeschichte* (salvation history), where God takes the initiative, as He always does, we concur with Dr. Paul Hiebert (1974:4) of the School of World Mission, Pasadena, that "conversion is an act of God. It is God building His kingdom in the lives of people." Throughout the course of *Heilsgechichte*, God has always been in search of lost humans. God's act, however, does not bypass humankind's moral capacity. On the contrary the Gospel appeals to the human will, demanding a response.

As individuals evaluate the options open to them, conversion can become a change of direction from a selfish way of life to new life in Christ (Augsburger 1970:87). Or, as William Barclay (1972:29) has said, "Conversion is the turn of the soul from things to God." Professor Bob Adams of Bogota, Colombia, defines conversion in *Diálago Teológico* (1973:83) as "the change affected by the Spirit of God in the life of a person who accepts divine intervention in his life and cooperates voluntarily with Him to bring about this change."

The many dimensions of life directly touched by conversion are beautifully delineated by the Methodist minister Robert Raines in his most inspiring book, *New Life in the Church* (1961:20 f.; 31 f.; 38 f.; 47 f.; 50 f.). He states that conversion begins in awakening, continues by the decision, matures by growth, endures in discipline, and takes place in *koinonia*. In all of these areas, God in His love, mercy, and grace is the Converter of persons insofar as they respond with their will to the divine will.

The basic meaning of the Latin term *convertere* is to turn or to change. Hence, to be converted in the spiritual sense means more than mere rational cognizance of, or mental consent to, Christian articles of faith, the recitation of a creed, or the adoption of a ritual. Spiritual conversion, in order to be deep and lasting in both temporal and spiritual life, means to be turned, changed, transformed, renewed, reborn, reconciled, and restored; it is a process which affects the total life-way of the convert. Therefore, says the Roman Catholic missiologist Louis J. Luzbetak,

> Conversion means a "turning" away from old ways to new ways, a basic reorientation in premises and goals, a wholehearted acceptance of a new set of values affecting the "convert" as well as his social group, day in and day out, twenty-four hours of the day and in practically every sphere of activity—economic, social, and religious. The change effected must become *living* parts of the cultural "organism" (1970:6).

Depending on the culture and social structure within which man lives, the conversion experience may be that of a people movement by caste, clan, tribe, or family making decisions by multi-personal actions; or it may be that of the individual persons who independently, and irrespectively of others, turn one by one from sin to forgiveness. The various case stories illustrate from actual life experiences how the different types and ways estranged and separated sinners convert and become reconciled people of God.

The Fourth World

To clarify the use of the term "Fourth World," it may be helpful, as Charles H. Kraft has suggested, to speak of four world categories, each having a political, an economic, a cultural, and a spiritual dimension.

The First World is politically democratic, economically capitalistic, and wealthy through free enterprise. Culturally Western, it is partially European and Anglo-American. Spiritually it is considered "Christian," at least nominally so. Until recently it was believed that geographically this world was made up of the North Atlantic arena of rich nations. But the current energy crisis of these countries on the one hand and the oil boom of Mideastern nations on the other is a clear indication that the geography of the truly wealthy countries is shifting.

The Second World is communistic and totalitarian in political structure with a socialistic, government-controlled economy. Its culture is either predominatly Western (Eastern Europe) or Chinese. Spiritually speaking, the communistic ideology—be that Russian Leninism or Chinese Moaism—is supposedly the religion of the masses, though many in Eastern Europe remain Christian.

We are by now also accustomed to speaking about the "Third World," comprising those nations and peoples of Africa, Asia, Latin America, and the Pacific Islands. They attained an independent economy, nationhood, and self-governing statehood, subsequent to the "Retreat of the West" since the end of World War II. Within a little over thirty years, this retreat is nearly complete. The former colonial empire builders of the democratic Occident no longer dominate the peoples and nations of the Orient. According to the roll call of the United Nations, the formerly *dominated* peoples of the "new world" now far outnumber the formerly *dominating* peoples of the "old world" (Winter, 1970:11-15). It appears as though the peoples of the Third World manifest a much stronger cohesiveness of nationalism and a more supreme loyalty of the individual to the nation-state than the peoples of former colonial powers (Kohn 1965:9). They no longer tolerate unjust dominance by the West.

Thus the Third World constitutes scores of politically younger independent nations who generally model their power structures after one of the democratic or communistic countries. The economy is often government-centered and the people are poor compared to those of the First and the Second World. Though the long colonial era has to an extent molded the culture of the Third World, the philosophical assumptions of its peoples have remained non-Western. Spiritually, they are adherents—at least by name—to one of the world's non-Christian religious systems, including animism.

The term "Fourth World" is at best an emerging concept. It has been suggested that it be used for the traditional segments of peoples of the First, Second, and Third World who are politically and economically uninvolved in, and unconcerned with, international affairs and economics. Culturally they are non-Western; and spiritually they are tribal, animistic, or syncretistic, though they are not interested in world movements, be they Christian or non-

Christian. In that sense the term may become useful.

In recent years, missiologists have begun to speak about the Fourth World in a somewhat different sense. (cf. Wagner, 1972:225; Ray, 1973:342; Stott, 1975:36). What is meant is the unevangelized, "the lost world," which consists of the more than 2,700 million unconverted people (Stott, 1975:36). All people everywhere who are not following Jesus Christ as Lord and, consequently, don't know or acknowledge Him as Savior from sin, constitute the Fourth World.

Economists also speak about a Fourth World which, according to the eminent professor of economy, Barbara Ward, is the world "that is about to fall off the edge of the global economy." World Vision President W. Stanley Mooneyham says that this world consists of about forty nations with one billion people who are "trying to exist on an average of twenty-seven cents a day" (Mooneyham, 1976:27; cf. Ostermann, 1975:16). These are "the poor nations" on the African, Asian, and Latin American continents that live "beyond the fringe of wealth" and, consequently, outside the circle of peoples who traditionally make up the central core of the North Atlantic arena of "the rich nations" (cf. Ward, 1962:86, 137; 1964:45 f.; 1966:74).

In the spiritual sense as used in this book, however, the Fourth World consitutes more like three billion people, regardless of their political ideology, economic wealth or poverty, geographical location within or without the North Atlantic arena of wealthy nations, and regardless of their religious adherence. The criterion here is not political, economic, and cultural, but spiritual; it is whether or not people know Jesus as Savior from sin and follow Him as Lord of life; it is whether or not they are a new people of God.

Thus conversion to Christ takes place in this Fourth

World, irrespective of cultural adherence, geographical distribution, religious persuasion, nominal Christian profession, ideological commitment, economic status or nationalistic loyalty. The message of the gospel is a call to all unevangelized people; it is a call to the unconverted to be converted and reconciled to God through Jesus Christ, the world's Savior and the Christian's Lord. The Holy Spirit makes that message of good news comprehensible and real.

Christian Ethnotheology

The ethnotheological approach to this process of change refers to the biblical principle that God the Creator is also God the Redeemer, and that He deals with humankind individually as well as collectively at the very level of its economic, social, cultural, and religious existence with the intent to forgive and reconcile. God wants to touch and change persons within their own cultural and sociological milieu. Conversion thus becomes the critical point at which the supra-cultural God meets with culture-bound humanity.

It is more than fifty years since Karl Barth (1886-1968), the eminent theologian of this century, wrote these perceptive words on the subject here referred to as "ethnotheology":

> We as theologians are supposed to speak about God. But we are human and are as such incapable of speaking about God. We are supposed to know both, what we ought to do and what we are incapable of doing, and by that very knowledge we are to bring honor to God. That is our dilemma. In comparison to this all else is child's play (Blaser, 1974:105, translation mine).

Those Barthian words are quoted by Klauspeter Blaser in his stimulating article on "Kommunikation des Evangeliums—Evangelium der Kommunikation," with the sub-

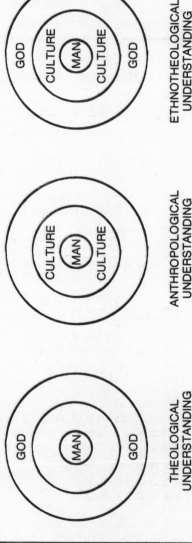

FIGURE 1: Understanding Christian Ethnotheology (Adapted by permission from Kraft 1973a: 116-118.)

THEOLOGICAL UNDERSTANDING

1. God created man in his own image. Man has the imago Dei within him.

ANTHROPOLOGICAL UNDERSTANDING

1. People of each culture create their own god(s) in their own image, or as an idealization of themselves.

ETHNOTHEOLOGICAL UNDERSTANDING

1. God created man in His image. Man perceives God in terms meaningful in his culture. This human perception will always be influenced by the imago Dei as well as by culture and sin.

2. God reveals himself to man in multiform ways.

3. Christainity is absolutely valid, but tends to be defined in Western philosophic terms.

4. Western culture is considered more Christian than other cultures.

5. Man is pervasively sinful, needing redemption.

2. Man thinks he receives communication from a supernatural source.

3. Christianity is but one of many valid cultural expressions of religion; hence no absolute model, only cultural by relative expressions of Christianity.

4. All cultures are vaild and relatively comparable to each other in terms of their ability to cope with reality.

5. Man is the product of his own culture. Redemption, if at all needed, is culturally determined.

2. God reveals himself to man in terms appropriate to man's cultural perception.

3. Supracultural Christianity is absolutely valid. It must be distinguished from its cultural expressions and transmitted apart from them.

4. All cultures are usable by God as vehicles for His interaction with man.

5. Culture is the vehicle of Satan as well as of God. Man and culture are pervasively sinful, needing redemption.

title "Observations on the Cultural Conditions of Theology." The thrust of the article is to create an awareness in the readers that the God whom they profess to worship reveals Himself within the cultural context of the worshipers. It is within the given matrix of the culture that the communication of the gospel can truly become the gospel of communication which aims at the conversion of women and men in the Fourth World.

The relatively new discipline of Christian ethnotheology has been developed by evangelical missiologists at such institutions as Wheaton College, The School of World Mission of Fuller Theological Seminary, Columbia Bible College, the former Kennedy School of Missions, and other. Dr. Charles Kraft of Fuller Theological Seminary defines Christian ethnotheology as a discipline "that takes both Christian theology and anthropology seriously while devoting itself to an interpretive approach to the study of God, man, and divine-human interaction" (Kraft, 1973a:110). From the one it derives its understanding of absolute and eternal truths, relating to God and His *salvific* plan for the total person; from the other it derives cultural and relative truths, relating to humankind and to its environment.

In the form of an equation it may be said that theology plus cultural ethnology (anthropology) equals Christian ethnotheology or $T + CE = CET$, demonstrated by Figure 1 on pages 30 and 31.

The purpose of ethnotheology is: (a) to understand more adequately humanity as God's creation and the *Imago Dei*, the abiding point of contact, in each person; (b) to become cognizant of the human cultural milieu and the complexities of humanity's alienation from its Creator; (c) to bring about a more balanced understanding of human life ways, attitudes, and relationships shaped not only by sin, but also by culture; (d) to discover more effective ways and means to communicate the gospel of Jesus Christ as the message of the supra-cultural God to culture-bound humanity so that persons might respond and be reconciled to their Creator and Redeemer. In the context of this study I will call the process of this response conversion, regeneration, or spiritual transformation.

PART II
Sin and Conversion in Biblical Context

Chapter 2

Light from the Old Testament

The whole story of God's redeeming purpose in history is restored unity.

—*Suzanne De Dietrich*, 1958

"The doctrine of conversion is written in bold letters across the pages of the Bible," writes professor G. W. Peters of Dallas (1963:235). According to Peters, "it is set forth with great emphasis in the Old Testament, is strongly reiterated in the Gospels, and boldly preached by the apostles." Thus the concept of conversion has deep roots in the biblical revelation of both testaments. Before the conversion concept can be dealt with, however, an underlying question emerges, namely the directional question of conversion *from* what *to* what, *from* whom *to* whom.

The assumption, of course, as pointed out earlier, is that Christian conversion implies a turning away from wrong to right, from the way of Satan to the way of God, from sin to forgiveness. This raises the additional question about the nature of sin, a subject the Bible treats with adequate clarity. The following story sheds light on both sin and conversion.

Case Story: The Fall and Return of a King

One late afternoon the king of the ancient people of God was overcome by lust of the flesh. He became involved with the wife of Uriah, one of his soldiers fighting the enemy. The king instructed his general to send the valiant warrior to the front lines, hoping he would be killed. Killed he was. Now the king felt at liberty to continue to live with the dead soldier's wife. Later on, however, he confessed that his sin was haunting him day and night (Psalm 32:3-4).

God sent a prophet to visit the king. "You have had Uriah killed by the sword of the Ammonites and taken his wife to be yours," said the fearless prophet. He continued by saying that the king had committed a threefold sin: first, adultery; second, murder; and third, he had given the Ammonites cause to blaspheme the God of the Israelites. "Therefore," the prophet declared, "the child to be born of Uriah's wife will not stay alive" (2 Samuel 11 and 12).

The king was shocked by these words of God's prophet. He admitted his guilt and responded: "I have sinned against the Lord." He asked God to forgive him his awful transgression and to cleanse him from his shameful and criminal acts. When the prophet left, the king made his experience of both sin and reconversion a public record. With a broken spirit he approached God with this prayer:

> Create in me a clean heart, O God, and grant me once again a new and steadfast spirit, that my thoughts may be pure and my desires right. Do not cast me away; do not banish me forever from your presence; do not deprive me altogether of your Holy Spirit. Restore to me again the joy of your salvation and help me to be obedient to you.

After this prayer the king made a covenant with God saying, "Then will I teach your ways to other sinners, and they—though they be guilty as I—will repent and be converted to you" (Psalm 51:1-13, paraphrased).

Sin in Relation to Conversion

In the context of this study, sin is seen as much in terms of its consequence—being that of separation or alienation from God the Creator and Redeemer—as in terms of the principal cause producing actual acts or steps leading to that state of alienation and to loss of meaning and identity. In our Western culture this condition generally is perceived as guilt; in some other cultures it may be fear, or shame, or any negative factor considered to be the dominant evil in a given culture. My reason for this view is the contention that conversion resolves the problem of alienation by reconciling man with God, regardless of what might be the cause of separation and alienation. Recognizing, then, that at the very basis there is a causative force, causing man to sin or act sinfully and to become estranged, a brief explanation of that very root or stem, process, and effect of the underlying problem seems imperative.

The Bible presents us with a rather comprehensive view of sin. The root meaning of what we call "sin" can be traced back to the Old Testament noun *chet*, sinfulness or being sinful, and the verb *chata*, to act sinfully. These words have their counterparts in the New Testament terms of *harmatia* and *harmatanein* respectively (cf. Bamberger, 1956:9).

There is a host of philological variations, etymological nuances, legal implications, and ethical and theological interpretations of the Old Testament sin concept. Kittel's *Theological Dictionary* and Vine's *Word Study* point out, however, that the basic and fundamental meaning of "all the variations indicate one and the same thing, namely, the deviation from a required norm which is the sense of the predominant root" of "to err" or "to stray" or "to miss the mark" (Kittel, 1964, 1:278; cf. Vine, 1948b, IV:32). Thus of the wayfarer in Proverbs 19:2 it is said, "He who makes haste with his feet misses his way" (RSV) or "goes astray" (Kittel 1964, 1:271). In keeping with this interpretation, I quote from one of England's great expositors of modern times, W. H. Griffith Thomas, who makes this observation on the word *sin* as it occurs in Romans 3:9:

> The various New Testament words for sin are deeply signifi-cant. The most familiar and frequent of them means "missing the mark"; another means "overstepping a boundary"; another, falling instead of standing; another, being ignorant instead of knowing; another, diminishing what should be rendered in full; another, disobeying a voice; another, disre-garding a command; another, willfully careless (1976:102).

The concept of sin, however, goes beyond observable ac-tion. It describes the very principle or "source of action, or an inward element producing acts"; it describes the very core of evil as organized power, acting through the members of the body, the organic instruments carrying out the action, though the seat of sin is in the will (Vine, 1948b, IV:32).

The effect sin has on people depends largely on their cultural orientation. In one society it will be a haunting guilt feeling; in another it may be perpetual fear; agonizing shame may be the phenomenon of a third. The results are similar in every case: alienation from God (in some societies from gods) and other people. To this I shall return later.

In summary sin, as understood in this study, is a combina-tion of the root, the stem, the branches, and the fruit of hu-mankind's rebellion against, and disobedience to, God. Sin is deviation from the right path; it is losing the intended course of direction and, consequently, missing the intended goal or end mark. Sin is transgression of God's law or violation of His expressed commandments (cf. Luther, 1951:169).

On the one hand, sin is alienation from God, on the other it is participation in acts of evil, dictated by "the prince of the power of the air, the spirit that is now at work in the sons of disobedience" (Ephesians 2:2). "In its ultimate consequences," says the late Anabaptist Bible scholar Jakob Kroeker (1842-1948), "sin is the very domain of the prince of darkness" (1949:109). As such, sin is the inspiration to evil attitude and action, resulting in *alienation from God through reversion;* acknowledgment of sin leads to confession and results in *reconciliation with God through conversion.*

The Old Testament Meaning of Conversion

In his excellent booklet, *Bekehrung und Wiedergeburt in biblischer Sicht,* Dr. Fritz Laubach (1957:6-8) traces the Hebrew verb *shuv* to 1,056 occurrences in the Old Testament, of which 118 are used strictly in a moral or religious context. The in-depth study of William Lee Holladay on *The Root Šûbh in the Old Testament* traces the verb to approximately 1,059 occurrences. Professor Holladay (1958:2) shows that the verb is basically one of motion but that this central meaning "branches out in manifold ways."

As already noted, in its function the verb *shuv* as such is neither sacred nor secular, but "absolutely neutral," as the Swiss theologian, Christoph Barth (1967:310), has pointed out. At the same time, however, it does convey the idea of our word conversion in its many applications and expresses the action of turning, returning, turning back, turning away, and giving back (cf. Peters, 1963:235-237; Laubach, 1954:6-8; Heikkinen, 1966:3). A more comprehensive definition of the term is presented by Barth:

The Hebrew verb *shuv* refers to the occurrence of "turning" in the opposite direction. The direction in which a man went or looked and which determined his plans and actions is changed into a new, the opposite direction. It means the "re-orientation" towards a goal from which one has moved away previously. Equally in relation both to concrete and abstract things, *shuv* indicates a "return"; geographically it means returning to a former position; circumstantially, it means "restoring" a former state (1967:310).

In theological understanding, *shuv* carries the idea of religious and ethical conversion in the sense of *turning* away from sin, *turning* to the Lord, *changing* one's course of direction, action, attitude, and relationship.

In this sense lies the relevancy of the concept for our study. A few examples will more clearly demonstrate the meaning of turning or conversion in the Old Testament context.

A *Key Passage from the Prophet*

In a special message given to Jeremiah by the Lord, the sins of the people of Judah are exposed and the fate of her leaders predicted. Jeremiah is to ask the people with words of lament why they have not returned to the ways of the Lord:

4b. When men fall, do they not rise again?
4c. If one turns away [shuv],
     does he not return [shuv]?
5. Why then has this people turned away [shuv]
    in perpetual backsliding [shuv]?
    They hold fast to deceit, they refuse to return [shuv].
6. I have given heed and listened, but they have not
    spoken aright; no man repents of his wickedness,
    saying, "What have I done?"
    Every one turns [shuv]

      to his own course, like a horse plunging
      headlong into battle.
      (Jeremiah 8:4b-6, structure mine.)

In these verses, the root form of *shuv* occurs six times. Like the pair of verbs "fall" and "rise" (v. 4b) describes opposites in a vertical direction, so the pair "turns" or "turn away" and "return" or "turn back" (v. 4c) implies opposites in horizontal direction. Verse 5 speaks more clearly to a convenantal relationship. Whether or not Jeremiah employs this technique as a mere play on words to indicate a juxtapositioning of opposite directions, both vertical and horizontal, is not quite clear (Holladay 1958:1). What is suggested, however—if not expressed—is physical motion, indicating infraction of covenantal relationship at one time and a mending of that relationship at another. According to Holladay (1958:2), "Jeremiah argues from the logical pattern of physical motion to a presumed pattern of religious relationship on the basis of the shared meanings embraced by the simple verb."

Furthermore, the Jeremiah text clearly states that the verb is used to describe a turning away from God "in perpetual backsliding"; it describes apostasy as well as a returning to God. This can be interpreted to mean that the one who turns away from God will again return to God. Jeremiah, in fact, implies that: "If one turns away from God, does he not return to God?" (Jeremiah 8:4c). This is also the interpretation given by Christoph Barth referred to earlier. Similarly, Holladay defines the verb *shuv* to mean once

      having moved in a particular direction, to move thereupon in
      the opposite direction, the implication being (unless there is
      evidence to the contrary) that one will arrive again at the initial
      point of departure (1958:53)

This is what God expects and desires. But Jeremiah makes it explicit in verse 6 that one may go on one's own sinful course "like a horse plunging headlong into battle"—and be lost.

General Conversion Passages

The biblical tradition of King James English (KJV) uses the word conversion more frequently than the newer translations. This can be seen in a comparison of the KJV with the Revised Standard Version (RSV): (a) Isaiah 6:10 is quoted four times in the New Testament (Matthew 13:15; Mark 4:12; John 12:40; Acts 28:27), saying, "Make the heart of this people fat, and make their ears heavy, and shut their eyes; lest they see with their eyes, and hear with their ears, and understand with their heart, and convert, and be healed." In the RSV the Isaiah passage, as well as three New Testament quotations of it, reads, "*turn*" and once (Mark 4:12), "turn again." (b) Isaiah 60:5 reads in the KJV: " . . . the abundance of the sea shall be converted unto thee, the forces of the Gentiles shall come unto thee." The RSV says that "the abundance of the sea shall be turned to you." (c) In Psalms 51:13, the KJV speaks of converting sinners, whereas the RSV says, "Then I will teach transgressors thy ways, and sinners will return to thee."

Forms of the same Hebrew verb are also used in 1 Samuel 7:3; Isaiah 55:7; Jeremiah 3:7; 25:5; 31:18; Ezekiel 18:23; Joel 2:12, and many other passages, translated in both the KJV and the RSV as "turn," "return," or "turn again."

Another word, though occurring less frequently, yet sometimes in parallel with *shuv*, is *niham* or *nicham*, meaning "to regret" or "to sigh." Whereas *shuv* is basically a word of motion, *nicham* is one of emotion as may be seen from Psalms 77:2; 90:13; 1 Samuel 15:29; Isaiah 1:24-26 (Heikkinen, 1966:3).

Turning from Sin to God

The implication of the verb "turning" often carries the meaning of "encounter," namely the encounter of people with their God as an expression of covenant renewal. This is particularly the case of the prophetic message. Jeremiah uses *shuv* in the covenantal sense 48 times (Holladay, 1958:128). Similarly, the word is used by Amos. When he calls on the people of Israel to prepare themselves to meet their God (4:12), he is, in fact, saying that God is simultaneously turning to them in judgment in order to bring about renewal of the covenant relationship. As God acts salvifically, people respond by turning to Him to renew their relationship with Him (cf. Hosea 6:1-3; Jeremiah 24:5-7).

Thus the act of "turning" or of "converting" on the part of the people from political powers, from false hopes, from futile involvements, and from false gods is their "ever new response to God's mighty acts" among them (Barth, 1967:311). In this process of turning, they encounter God; at the point of encounter, they are faced with a verdict, as the experience of Elijah and God's people on Mount Carmel vividly demonstrates (1 Kings 18:1-39). When Elijah and his people met God on His terms, God acted redemptively on their behalf.

In a stimulating essay on "Conversion in an Ecumenical Context," Dr. Paul Löffler (1967b:256-257) states categorically that "God's action in history demands concrete response by historic persons" and that conversion in the Old Testament context means "the re-turn to the covenant." In the Old Testament context, return may be individualistic or collective, but it always must be *personal*. "A converted individual," professor Nikos A. Nissiotis of the Church of Greece correctly observes, "passes from his autonomy as an individual to dependency in that he is a person returning to an

established relationship with God" (1967:264). But this personal return to God is to be understood "as an indication and
representation of the 'return' of the whole people" of Israel
(Christoph Barth, 1967:310; 311); it is a resolute return to a
renewal of their covenant with their God and a renewal of
the covenant community of the people of God in a changed
world.

This observation has significant implications on the principle of a people movement to Christ, a principle developed
and dealt with extensively by the so-called "Church Growth
School of Thought" of the Fuller Theological Seminary
School of World Mission. Although it is beyond the scope of
this study, I will have occasion below to make reference to
this principle and its importance for an ethnotheological
understanding of conversion as a missiological concern.

Chapter 3

The New Testament Unfolding of Conversion Concepts

God's act was always a challenge to decision and commitment, and man's response the portrayal of his inner state.
—*G. Ernest Wright*, 1969.

The writers of the New Testament were masters of communication. They used comparable terms to convey the
content of the message from the Old Testament so that the
message would be meaningful to the audience of their time.
This is what ethnolinguists call the "principle of dynamic
equivalence" (cf. Wonderley, 1968:51). Thus for the Hebrew words *shuv* and *nicham* they used a variety of terms,
all indicating the idea of changing one's course of action or
direction and becoming different persons (cf. Barclay,
1972:23-24; Preuschen, 1910:438; Arndt and Gingrich,
1952:301; Friedrich, 1971,VII:714-729).

Case Story: The Conversion of a Tramp

One day there was great jubilation in a certain oriental
family. The occasion was the homecoming of the youngest

son. The story is told by a great Teacher whom religious
leaders accused of associating with sinners (Luke 15:1-3).

> And he said, "There was a man who had two sons; and the
> younger of them said to his father, 'Father, give me the share of
> property that falls to me.' And he divided his living between
> them. Not many days later, the younger son gathered all he had
> and took his journey into a far country, and there he squan-
> dered his property in loose living. And when he had spent
> everything, a great famine arose in that country, and he began
> to be in want. So he went and joined himself to one of the
> citizens of that country, who sent him into his fields to feed
> swine. And he would gladly have fed on the pods that the swine
> ate; and no one gave him anything. But when he came to
> himself he said, 'How many of my father's hired servants have
> bread enough and to spare, but I perish here with hunger! I will
> arise and go to my father, and I will say to him, "Father, I have
> sinned against heaven and before you; I am no longer worthy
> to be called your son; treat me as one of your hired servants." '
> And he arose and came to his father. But while he was yet at a
> distance, his father saw him and had compassion, and ran and
> embraced him and kissed him. And the son said to him,
> 'Father, I have sinned against heaven and before you; I am no
> longer worthy to be called your son.' But the father said to his
> servants, 'Bring quickly the best robe, and put it on him; and
> put a ring on his hand, and shoes on his feet; and bring the fat-
> ted calf and kill it, and let us eat and make merry; for this my
> son was dead, and is alive again; he was lost, and is found.' And
> they began to make merry." Luke 15:11-24.

External Action and Motion Concepts

The words employed to tell the conversion story
throughout history are many. In fact, professor Georg
Bertram of Giessen lists ten basic terms from which he
proceeds to analyze and interpret the New Testament concept of conversion (Friedrich, 1971, VII:714 f.). The most
important of these for the purpose of this study are the root

strephein and the compound words *epistrephein, apostrep-hein,* and *anastrephein.* Although they do not only describe external motion, they all carry the idea of turning around in either the physical, mental, moral, or spiritual sense (cf. Barclay, 1972:20; Laubach, 1954;7-10; Rienecker, 1967:195-96). Thus the verbs are to be understood in the sense of being more *motive* than *emotive* in their causal function.

More specifically, *strephein* is used transitively as well as intransitively. The fundamental meaning, however, in both usages is "to twist," or "to turn," or "to bend," or "to steer" (Friedrich, 1971, VII:714). Following Numbers 14:3, deacon Stephen used the verb in Acts 7:39 for an inward turning of the heart of the Jewish fathers back to Egypt. Then "God turned away and delivered them up to serve the host of heaven" (Acts 7:42, NASB) and therewith directed them toward or turned them over to stellar powers. In Acts 13:46, the apostles Paul and Barnabas are said to be turning away from their own people, the Jews, to the Gentiles because the former rejected the message, whereas the latter rejoiced to receive it.

The compound verb *epistrephein* occurs nearly forty times in the New Testament, with about half that number in Luke's writings alone. "Again about a half have a spatial reference and denote physical movement" (Friedrich, 1971, VII:726). Thus when God's angel appeared to Zechariah, the angel said that John the Baptist would be instrumental in *turning* or *converting* "many of the sons of Israel to the Lord their God" (Luke 1:16). In a message to Simon Peter, Christ said: "When you have *turned again* [or have been converted], strengthen your brethren" (Luke 22:32). When Peter had experienced that *turning again* he did, indeed, challenge others to do the same by saying: "Repent *[meta-noesate]* therefore, and turn again *[epistrephate]*, that your

sins may be blotted out" (Acts 3:19). Commenting on this
verse, Ernst Haenchen observes that Peter here combines
the concepts *repent* and *return* to express one single great
move, namely that of

> "turning" which leads a Gentile or a Jew to God and to faith in
> the Kyrios Jesous. Since God offers the possibility of such a
> change of heart, Peter and John can call on men to return.
> Where, as in the present verse, the two concepts are found
> together, *metanoein* will express more the turning away from
> evil, *epistrephein* on the other hand, the positive new direction,
> the turning to God and his *Kyrios* (cf. 20, 21), and the new way
> of life (26). This conversion leads to "life" (5, 31), to the forgive-
> ness of sins (1971:208).

The other two compounds mentioned above, *apostrep-*
hein and *anastrephein,* both carry the idea of turning and
changing. The former, however, has reference to moral
conduct, whereas the latter implies more the way toward
such types of conduct. That becomes particularly clear in the
New Testament Epistles. Paul calls on the Ephesian readers
"to put off the old man with his *walk* in deceitful lusts"
(Ephesians 4:22). Peter reminds the members of the new
community of believers that they are redeemed from their
vain *walk* which they inherited from their fathers (1 Peter
1:18). This *walk* or *conduct,*Paul writes to Timothy (1
Timothy 1:12), is as much a special "gift of Christians along
with possession of the word, love, faith, and holiness"
(Friedrich, 1971, VII:721).

Among the many other references recording conversion
words are Matthew 13:14; Mark 4:12; Acts 9:35; 11:21;
14:15; 15:19; 26:18; 28:27; 2 Corinthians 3:16; 1 Thessa-
lonians 1:9; James 5:19-20; 1 Peter 2:25; cf. Matthew 18:3;
Acts 15:3.

Internal Emotive and Experiential Concepts

In addition to the words that indicate a turning away from sin toward God or from a vain walk to a holy conduct, there are a number of terms which deal with accompanying phenomena, describing the very essence of conversion.

One of these words is *metanoein,* to repent, already referred to in the Acts 3:19 passage. The German theologian Ralf Luther explains *metanoein* to mean *umdenken* (literally, to think in reverse); or to let one's thoughts, which always were opposing God's will, move far beyond what one has normally thought up to the present moment. It means to break through the physical perimeter to the metaphysical where man learns to think in harmony with God's will (Luther, 1951:21-22). Thus the basic meaning of the term is, as the case story of this chapter illustrates, "to have a change of mind, it being an altered attitude toward sin." What this means, says Dr. D. Edmund Hiebert (1975:1), professor of New Testament at the Biblical Seminary in Fresno, is " 'an aftermind,' for upon repentance the attitude to and view of sin is different." Repentance involves a change of the total person—mind, heart, and will. "It means to take a new direction in life. It means to give up the old life and enter upon the new life" (Raines, 1961:43).

As in the case story of the tramp, spiritual turning has deep moral implications. Only as man repents of his sin, the basic problem of his alienation, can he experience conversion or regeneration, which is the new birth (John 3:1-8; Acts 2:38). That is why Peter calls his "brethren in the flesh" unequivocally to repent (Acts 2:38; 3:19). Paul demands that Jews and Gentiles alike repent (Acts 26:20). The Scripture says that God "commands all men everywhere to repent" (Acts 17:30);

With these terms, the New Testament kerygma rises to its

climatic issue with the commanding appeal to turn to God: *metanoete*. Thus *metanoia*, says Dr. Jacob W. Heikkinen (1967:315) of the Lutheran Theological Seminary, "is the keyword symbolizing the character of the response on the part of men to the preaching of the judgement and the rule of God."

A second word which describes the inner process is *homologein*, to confess. The tramp in our case story demonstrated this by saying, "Father, I have sinned." *Homologein* is a compound verb which literally means, "to say the same thing." Whenever there is confession of sin, the person doing the confessing is in agreement with God's verdict about that sin. "He is willing to call sin what God calls sin, giving it its true name, not some high-sounding euphemism that hides the hideous character of sin" (Hiebert, 1975:1). Thus confession becomes an integral part of conversion.

Paul makes a strong case for confessing Jesus as Lord. In fact, he makes salvation contingent on confession (Romans 10:9). The Apostle John, like King David (Psalms 32:1-5), makes confession a condition for forgiveness and cleansing (1 John 1:9). Jesus Himself places high priority on confessing in this life and in the life to come (Matthew 10:32-33). Confession of sin on the one hand, and confession of Christ as Lord on the other, are both psychologically and theologically sound. "The divine impression man experiences in conversion," says the Wiedenest Bible teacher Hans Legiehn (1954:69), "must find human expression to attest that experience."

A further concept that expresses what happens at the turning experience is *pisteuein*, "to believe" or "to have faith." This does not simply mean to lend credence to some*thing*, but to place full confidence, trust, or reliance in some*one* (cf. Vine, 1943:I, 116-17). The New Testament scholar William Barclay points out that faith is central to conversion. The jailor at Philippi was told to believe in the Lord Jesus Christ in order to be saved (Acts 16:31). The early converts became members of the church because they believed and trusted in the Word. They believed that in turning away from sin to God the Forgiver, they actually entered into a new relationship; by faith they exchanged estrangement for reconciliation (cf. Barclay, 1972:53). Luther's maxim of *sola fide* (faith alone) in Christ is still biblical bedrock in the evangelistic kerygma that calls for conversion. For "faith cometh by hearing, and hearing by the word of God." And again: "Whoever believes in Him shall not be ashamed" (Romans 10:11; 17). But this believing is more than mere mental consent to, or verbal recital of, a creed; it is full reliance on a Person, the Person of Jesus Christ, Savior *and* Lord.

Justification—Divine/Human Interaction

There is one other concept that merits attention for understanding conversion. Because of its importance, it deserves separate treatment. It is the concept conveyed by the English word "justification." That concept is closely linked to the previous one, namely "faith," and together they form the core of the Pauline theology of "justification by faith" (Romans 8).

The word *dikaiosis* or *dikaios*, justification, is a legal term which "denotes the act of pronouncing righteous" (Vine, 1948, Vol. II:284). It is *pistis*, faith, that brings man into the outworking atonement and salvation; but it is *dikaios* that takes man up into the righteousness of God.

A key passage for our consideration is Romans 4:25—5:1. The issue is justification by faith. The one is God's part, the other man's. In two symmetrical clauses, Paul sums up the almost mysterious relationship the *believing* convert enters into with the *justifying* Converter. Between the two stands Jesus Christ, the crucified and risen Mediator:

> He was delivered up because of our transgression;
> He was raised up because of our justification. (cf. Romans 4:25; NASB).

The great New Testament scholar, Adolf Schlatter (1852-1938), has very beautifully presented the relationship between God and us through Christ. Through Christ, he says, God has made something of us what we could not be by ourselves:

> Through Christ God manifests to us two things: our call and our justification, our death and our life. As we behold the cross of Christ, we must view ourselves as transgressors; because it was on our behalf that He died. As we behold the resurrection of Christ, we must view ourselves as justified; because it was on our behalf that God raised the Prince of Life from the dead (1948:91, translation mine).

Over the shed blood of the *dying* Christ on the cross, God pronounced justification in favor of guilty humanity and thus annulled human condemnation that brought Him to the cross; over the empty tomb of the *risen* Christ God pronounced Christ's resurrection so that we might be justified and brought to life. "Such is the bond of solidarity framed by the plan of God between Christ and us," observes the respected commentator Frederick Godet (1812-1900). "Our lot is as it were, interwoven with His: we sin, He dies; we are justified, He lives again" (Godet, 1956:184).

On the basis of his arguments in Romans 4, Paul continues in 5:1 to describe the result of our justification by faith:

> Since, then, we have obtained by means of faith our sentence of justification from God, we find ourselves transferred relatively to Him into a state of peace, which henceforth displaces in our minds the fear of wrath (Godet, 1956:186).

These words describe the transition from non-faith to faith, from not being justified to being justified. Faith, in the sense of trust, is the human side of accepting God's offer of salvation; justification is God's side of sealing that acceptance. The result of this dual action is peace between the believer and God the Justifier.

In an attempt to convey more clearly the death-resurrection axis on the one hand and the justification-faith axis on the other, we portray these Pauline concepts in a diagram (Figure 2 on page 56).

The experience of justification—God's part—and of faith—our part—is, I propose, the very moment when conversion has happened and sanctification has begun. The convert has become a child of God who now embarks on the New Way, the way of sonship under the Fatherhood of God; the way of discipleship under Christ's lordship; the way of body life in fellowship under Christ's headship; the way of Christian growth and sanctification in the believers' church under the Holy Spirit's tutorship, and the way of witness and service under the Spirit's leadership.

Observations on the Biblio-Theological Concepts

The above exegetical references on the understanding and unfolding of the biblical meaning of conversion call for a few additional observations.

The words used in Scripture to describe what we call "Christian conversion" and "regeneration" indicate the idea of turning or changing one's course of action, direction, at-

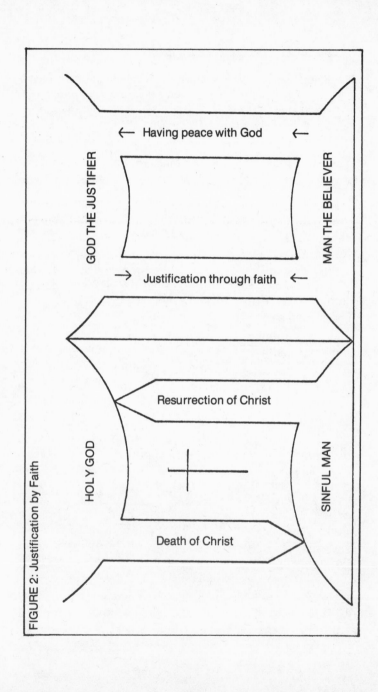

FIGURE 2: Justification by Faith

GOD THE JUSTIFIER

MAN THE BELIEVER

← Having peace with God ←

→ Justification through faith ←

HOLY GOD

SINFUL MAN

Resurrection of Christ

Death of Christ

titude, and relationship. They contain both motional and emotional qualities, ranging widely in terms of implicit nuances and explicit effects on man's behavioral pattern. Moreover, from the study of these and other conversion words, it becomes evident that they are interrelated. Confessing and believing in terms of trust (Romans 10:9-10) express a new relationship and a change of allegiance from the former self-life to a life of discipleship under the lordship of the risen Christ. At other times, repentance and conversion are placed side by side, as in Acts 3:19 and 26:20. In Acts 11:21, believing and conversion are expressed as belonging together. Again, in Acts 20:21 Paul calls both Jews and Greeks to "repentance toward God and faith in our Lord Jesus Christ" (NASB). The Apostle John even goes so far as to suggest that believing in Christ's name, being born of God, and receiving Jesus into one's life are an integral part of the same experience (John 1:12; 6:37). Therein lies the Christological basis of a New Testament theology of conversion.

Furthermore, a reading of the conversion passages makes it clear that God is the Originator and Initiator of the conversion act and process. The sovereign God appeals to our free will. But we are saved by grace and justified through faith. This we dare not forget. As Yahweh once chose Israel to become His partner in covenant, so He still chooses people to become His partners in the new covenant. He calls people to forsake sin and turn to Him; He commands them to be converted; He warns them of judgment if they fail to listen and obey His call and command; He promises to forgive their sins and to restore them from a life of alienation to a life of harmony and fellowship (cf. Peters, 1963:236). In all of this, however, people must of their own will respond to God's sovereign initiatory acts of call and appeal. The ancient aphorism still holds: "A man convinced against his will is of the same opinion still." "In no case," contend Hogg and Vine (1959:44), "is God, or Christ, or the Holy Spirit, said to turn, or convert, anyone. Conversion is always the voluntary act of the individual in response to the presentation of truth."

It is also significant to observe that the New Testament apostles and other witnesses did a tremendous job of translating Old Testament concepts from the Hebrew culture into the Hellenistic soul and mind. Not only did they translate words such as *shuv* and *nicham,* but they put coherent ideas into a new dress and meaning, as Michael Green (1975:115) has pointed out. "Without such a task of translation the message would have been heard, perhaps, but not assimilated."

In all of this, however, the role of the Holy Spirit should not be underestimated. Recall our Lord's words to His disciples on this matter:

> And when he [the Holy Spirit] comes, he will convince the world of sin and of righteousness and of judgment: of sin, because they do not believe in Me; of righteousness, because I go to the Father, and you will see Me no more; of judgment, because the ruler of this world is judged, John 16:18-11.

The key role of the Holy Spirit in conversion is that of convincing and convicting unconverted people everywhere the gospel is preached, that they must be converted. This particular work of the divine Spirit is a process by which people come to realize that they are wrong in their relationship, attitude, and thinking with respect to three great biblical, religious, and moral truths. In the first place, the Holy Spirit convicts people that there is such a thing as *sin*, and that the very core of it is persistent unbelief in relation to

Jesus Christ. J. Oswald Sanders calls such unbelief "the parent of all sin" (1974:41), and refers to it as the real issue between the unsaved and the saving God. Second, the Holy Spirit convicts people that there is such a thing as *righteousness* which was embodied in the incarnate Christ, manifested in the crucified Savior, demonstrated by the risen Lord, and "attested by His return to heaven." Third, it is also the Holy Spirit who convicts the world of the fact that there is a *judgment* "which consists in the triumph through Christ of righteousness over sin and Satan" (Sanders, 1974:39-41). That is to say that Satan no longer can claim to hold people captive; they are redeemed from his power through Christ's death and resurrection, the divine act which makes once sinful persons who now believe, righteous and acceptable before a holy and just God.

Moreover, just as conversion involves a vertical response to God's message, so it results in the converted being involved with others. The test of conversion is obedience to God and service to others and society. The fruit of the Spirit *through* the converted is the manifestation of the work of the Holy Spirit *in* those who are converted. The German church statesman, Dr. Paul Löffler, offers this commentary on conversion:

> In the Old Testament the prophetic call to conversion always includes an emphatic, "No!" to idolatry. In the New Testament conversion sets men free to a new life in Christ. It is acceptance of forgiveness, based on obedience of faith. Such liberation has not only to do with sins, the moral wrong and evil deeds of men, it equally concerns the forces of society and the cosmic powers of the universe (1967b:257).

Finally, conversion always involves people. It involves both sinners and saints. It involves the world and the church.

It involves Christ, the *Kyrios* (Lord) and Head of the church. It involves His disciples who are the members of His body.

Although I will address this question later, it should be remembered that God uses the believers' church as His medium or channel to work for conversion in the world, but also as a fold or gathering place for the converted from the world. The church provides the converts with a place for fellowship, communion, and love; it gives them a place for worship, edification, and growth; it offers them opportunities for expression, sharing, and service; it involves them in hearing God's Word corporately, in praying to God unitedly, in learning from God and from each other in community. Here the converts become aware what it means to be disciples and learners under the lordship of Christ. Here they discover their Head and His members, their "gifts and graces" in the body of Christ, as Arnold Bittlinger (1967) has put it in a book title. In *Life Together*, Dietrich Bonhoeffer (1906-1945) has called it a privilege "to live in visible fellowship with other Christians. It is by the grace of God" Bonhoeffer attested, "that a congregation is permitted to gather visibly in the world to share God's Word and sacrament" (1954:18).

Summary

When speaking of Christian conversion in the biblical context, it is imperative to remember that the concept of sin or its equivalent must be clearly understood within the sociocultural framework of a given society, lest our understanding of conversion remain forever nebulous. Regardless of how sin is viewed by theologians and scientists, it is a violation of God's norms, resulting in human separation and alienation from the Creator through reversion and waywardness. Acknowledgement and confession of sin, however, leads persons to reconciliation with their Maker and Redeemer through conversion. Such is the message of the above case stories—that of a king and that of a tramp.

Thus the meaning of conversion in both Testaments is basically one of change and turning. In its positive sense, it means a return of the wayward sinner to the waiting, forgiving Father. A person who converts changes a course of direction and action, values and attitudes, relationships and total lifeway. Once a person rationally and volitionally responds to God's call to return to our Maker and Redeemer, that person experiences *motion* in terms of external, directional change and *emotion* in terms of internal, attitudinal change. The Holy Spirit performs the work of regeneration and the individual becomes a new creation.

As each person repents and confesses sin, God forgives and reconciles the erring one to Himself. As one puts his trust in Christ the Savior, God justifies the believing convertee. The crucified and risen Mediator, Christ Jesus as Lord, always stands between holy God and sinful humanity. He manifests to us both our condemnation as unbelievers and our justifications as believers. In the light of the crucified Savior on the cross, we see our sinfulness and thus our lostness; in the light of the risen Lord from the grave we behold our forgiveness and thus our foundness. Because of our sin, Christ died; because God raised Him to life, we are justified.

Thus the death-resurrection axis of Christ becomes meaningful only when we see it against the justification-faith axis that brings God and sinner into a new Father-son relationship. It is at this point where the life of discipleship begins to unfold under the lordship of Jesus Christ until the disciple reaches the stature of his Master. The setting for such growth and maturation, Christian discipline and sanctification is that "body life" where the members share their gifts and graces in mission and ministry for the benefit of all; it is that "life together," that "incendiary fellowship" where the believers become visible and irresistible to the people of the Fourth World.

PART III
Conversion Concerns in the Ethnotheological Matrix

Chapter 4

Empirical and Experiential: A Psychological Concern

> Our experience of the gospel does not make the gospel true,
> but it does confirm that the gospel makes a difference today.
> —*Fisher Humphreys*, 1976

From the psychological vantage point, the question is raised whether the conversion experience is sudden or gradual; whether it is an event or a process; whether it is a relatively smooth process or a rough pilgrimage; whether it is one single experience or a series of peak-experiences. The matter becomes even more complex when we combine the known types and look at the variety of possibilities emerging from such a combination. Thus conversion may be an individual or a group action; it may be a dramatic, sudden crisis experience or a gradual process; it may be sudden in one case and gradual in another; it may be one crisis or a series of crises. No two individual conversions are exactly alike; no two movements toward Christ on the part of one person are the same. Similar principles, however, may be operative in all of them, leading men and women to a point in time when each personally can confidently say, "I am *now* a child of God."

Three Case Stories°

These conversion stories will illustrate the principles operative in the models or types discussed at length later in this chapter.

Case Story A: The Conversion of a Weaver in Brazil

I was standing close to a weaving machine, watching the intricate work of the instrument fashioning the warp and the woof until a sizable roll of fine cotton fabric was ready for release. The man on the chair was Mr. Adolf Stinshoff, the owner of the factory in Blumenau, Brazil. The Stinshoffs were regular participants in our worship services and Bible study meetings in the church where I was pastor.

"So it was in my life," Mr. Stinshoff said, as we discussed the analogy between the work of the weaving machine and God's work in man's life. "God is a Master Weaver. I grew up under the influence of godly parents," he continued as we walked to the house to join Mrs. Stinshoff for morning coffee. "God spun and weaved until I was prepared to consciously assume the role of discipleship."

"But how did you experience conversion?" I queried. "Conversion? I don't know," he replied. Then he added, "I know when I was baptized, but I know neither time nor place of conversion. In fact, I don't even know of an experience which I can call my conversion to Christ. What I do know is that I am a child of God through Jesus Christ my Lord, and I rejoice in His service."

Whoever has had the occasion to associate with Mr. Stinshoff as I did will not doubt his assertion.

°Case Story B was written upon my request by the convertee, Mr. Cornelius Ott, December 23, 1976. Mr. Ott now lives in Colônia Nova, near Bagé in Rio Grande do Sul, Brazil. Translation mine. Original script on file.

Case Story B: The Conversion of a Medic in Russia

I had spent three years as a medic on the Turkish front during World War I. When I was released, I went back to my home in Russia.

Although my parents gave me a comfortable bed and good food, I could neither sleep nor eat. The words of a dying soldier on the battlefield haunted me day and night: "Kardash su wirasim" ("Brother, give me water"). Instead of giving him to drink, I deprived him of a wooden spoon and a piece of soap. My parents thought my problem was due to a love affair, but it was a guilty conscience.

Then on a Sunday night, June 18th, God sent me a Sunday school teacher. This man had become burdened about my spiritual condition. He invited me to go for a walk with him. I lit a cigarette. As we came to the forest, he revealed his purpose of coming and asked me whether I wanted to be converted. I responded affirmatively, but insisted that I could not be saved because of the great sin in my life, particularly the episode on the battlefield.

My friend counseled with me, read various portions of Scripture, and pointed to God's word in Isaiah 1:18: "Though your sins are like scarlet, they shall be as white as snow; though they are red like crimson, they shall become as wool."

We knelt right there on the road. My friend prayed and asked me to pray too. I had no words; I could not pray. Then, finally, I cried to God. My heart was in agony. God forgave me. Now I felt relief; my burden was gone, and I could thank God for forgiveness.

As we got up from our knees, a group of young men approached us. God gave me courage to tell them of my conversion experience and to ask whether they wanted to be converted as well. Most of them disappeared, but two were converted. That resulted in a great revival in our village.

Case Story C: The Conversion of a Psychiatrist in Japan

"When I was a medical student at the university, I had my first encounter with Christianity," related the Japanese psychiatrist, Dr. Tetsuo Kashiwagi, before an audience in a Fresno, California, church on July 27, 1975. "My girlfriend invited me to Christian meetings," Kashiwagi continued. "The people there impressed me. They seemed to possess a sense of security and displayed a spirit of serenity which I liked, but lacked."

As the people listened to Kashiwagi's fascinating story, and expected him to climax it by telling them of a sudden, cataclysmic conversion experience, the speaker said, "My conversion took five years during which I read the Bible, first sporadically, then more regularly. Each time I attended a Christian worship service or read the Bible, I experienced a change in my life; each experience was a kind of climax. Finally, I decided to be baptized. I asked the pastor to hold me down as long as possible. I stayed under water eighty seconds, as my fiancée told me, and prayed for forgiveness of sins. When I stepped out of the water, I knew that I was a newborn man."

Gleanings from Psychology

Conversion is an empirical happening, profoundly affecting both the rational as well as the emotional, the relational as well as the behavioral aspects of one's lifestyle.

A Jamesian Definition of Conversion

In his frequently quoted classical—though not necessarily theological—definition of religious conversion, the father of American pragmatic philosophy, William James (1842-1910), wrote in his famous Gifford Lectures (1901-1902):

To be converted, to be regenerated, to receive grace, to experience religion, to gain assurance, are so many phrases which denote the process, gradual or sudden, by which a self

> hitherto divided, and consciously wrong, inferior and unhappy, becomes unified and consciously right, superior and happy, in consequence of its firmer hold upon religious realities (James, 1905:189).

The adjectival clause, "gradual or sudden," accents the key significance of the definition, pointing out the nature and process of the experience.

The ABC's of Conversion Types

Following professor E. D. Starbuck's *Psychology of Religion* (1899), James presupposes two types of religious experience, placed here in this order: (a) "the volitional type" and (b) "the self-surrender type" (James, 1905:207-208). I would like to suggest a third model: (c) the "peak-experience type." This model combines the two Jamesian types, but gives rise to a distinctly third one, dealt with by Professor Abraham Maslow, as will be pointed out later. Hereafter, these types will be referred to as Type A, Type B, and Type C, corresponding to case stories A, B, and C, respectively.

(A) Volitional and Gradual

James (1905:206) describes Type A as a "conscious and voluntary way" or the gradual "regenerative change" which "consists in the building up, piece by piece, of a new set of moral and spiritual habits." The final step in this process, James maintains (1905:210), is one of falling back "on the larger Power that makes for righteousness, which has been welling up in his own being, and lets it finish in its own way the work it has begun."

This principle of gradualism in conversion is illustrated by Case Story A at the beginning of this chapter about the experience of the Weaver in Brazil.

(B) Sudden Self-Surrender

What is referred to in this study as "Type B" conversion, James (1905:217) described as "those instantaneous instances . . . in which . . . a complete division is established in the twinkling of an eye between the old life and the new." A good example is the prodigal son's experience, recorded in Luke 15. When he "came to himself," he made a sudden turnabout, walking in the opposite direction, back to his home. So it was with the medic, whose conversion is recorded in Case Story B.

The effects of this type of experience are more abundant than those of Type A, and often quite startling. Of the many illustrations, James cites the experience of Paul as one of the most eminent examples of the cataclysmic, sudden disruptive, subconscious or "subliminal" self-surrender types of conversion. Yet he goes on to say that "the difference between the two types is after all not radical" (James, 1905:208).

Despite the fact that he sees no radical difference between the two types, his subsequent lengthy analysis of the two happenings clearly favors the sudden crisis experience which he identifies with mystical experience. "One may truly say," states James, "that personal religious experience has its roots and center in the mystical states of consciousness" (James, 1905:380). Both the mystical experience and the self-surrender type of conversion are sudden, instantaneous, as Walter Clark in his Jamesian studies has pointed out:

> A mystical experience *per se* does not come gradually to a person's consciousness over a period of two or three days or years, but, within the space of a few minutes, or perhaps the twinkling of an eye, it is *there*, just as the new light of a conversion experience. Then the mystical experience with its new knowledge and new values may bring what amounts to conver-

sion along with it. At least this is what seems to have happened with Socrates, Isaiah, St. Paul, St. Francis, Teresa of Avila, Ignatius of Loyola, Pascal, R. M. Bucke, and Arthur Koestler, to name just a few (Clark, 1965:35).

(C) Peak Experiences

More recent studies of conversion have shown that James's concept of "the sudden event" may, in fact, also consist of a series of sudden, climactic events, described by professor Abraham Maslow (1964:59) as "peak-experiences," which I have referred to as "Type C." These experiences, according to Maslow (1964:61-62), are "religious happenings" which seem "to lift us to greater than normal heights so that we can see and perceive in a higher than usual way." James (1905:189) wrote that the conversion experience results in a state of being right, superior, happy, and whole with a "firmer hold upon religious realities."

Maslow (1964:62-63) makes similar assertions about the peak-experiences which make the experiencers "larger, greater, stronger, bigger, taller people" who come to feel that "life is worthwhile or ... meaningful." "Only after a long and difficult conflict with their inner motives," writes Billy Graham (1967:279), do these people come to peace with God and themselves and achieve the desired equilibrium in conversion.

This "peak-experience" type is illustrated by Case Story C, the conversion of Dr. Tetsuo Kashiwagi of Osaka, Japan. As stated above, his conversion had taken five years from the initial encounter with Christianity until the point of his baptism. Only upon his baptismal experience, Kashiwagi attested, had he known for the first time that he had become a new person. He told the audience that the conversion of his mother had taken seven years. "It was a long and hard struggle for her," Kashiwagi noted.

Observations and Reflections

The Jamesian analysis of religious experience demands additional comments, touching both weaknesses and strengths.

Weaknesses in James's Delineations

James's definition has several limatations. One is its narrow applicability to only individualistic, Western cultures. In many non-Western communal societies the conversion experience happens collectively, yet multi-individually or multi-personally, as I will show below. This factor is altogether overlooked by James.

Another limitation is its failure to distinguish the gradual process of conversion from the dramatic event. He has amalgamated and homogenized the two experiences and thus intensified rather than clarified the dilemma. We should also note that James deals exclusively with two types of religious experiences. Thus he not only restricts the conversion experience to types A and B, but also contradicts his own book title which proposes to treat *The Varieties of Religious Experience*.

Values in James's Definition

The main value of the definition given by James is the proposition from which neither the evangelical revivalist nor the social anthropologist would dissent. The former sees conversion as "a personal revolution" (Graham, 1967:271); the latter sees it as spiritual maturation (Fergeson, 1965:14) and cultural transformation (Wallace, 1970:195). Both, however, would affirm with James, "If any man is converted he is a new creation; the old things have passed away; all things have become new" (Fergeson, 1965:14). The late E. Stanley Jones (1884-1973) has affirmed the totality of conversion by saying that "conversion transforms everything it touches, and it touches everything" (1953:153). That is certainly in keeping with James's concept.

James also helps us to understand the dynamics in operation at conversion. Religious conversion may be a sudden event in one case and a gradual process in another, as James's own analysis of his definition points out. In the instantaneous event, the Holy Spirit seems to compress the operative psychodynamics into one short span of time with or without the accompanying phenomenon of a trance or ecstasy-experience. Sometimes this may happen in a "twinkling of an eye," as James put it; sometimes it may last for several hours or days. The experiences of the prophet Isaiah (Isaiah 6) and the Apostle Paul (Acts 9:3f.) illustrate this.

Exceptions to James's Views

From a philosopher's perspective, even Socrates is said to have experienced an ecstatic conversion of the sudden type (Taylor, 1952:47-48) which marked a turning point in his life and activity (Nock, 1964:165-166). To identify the philosophical concept and the stoic's experience of conversion with Christian conversion and regeneration, however, as Nock and Taylor seem to do, is an unwarranted assumption. Conversion from sin to Christ as Lord and conversion from one philosophic system to another are two very different types of conversion, as Michael Green (1975:144-48) demonstrates. The psychological principles operative may be similar, but the results achieved are quite different.

Although in the end result James (1905:207-208) sees no great difference between Type A (Volitional) and Type B (Self-surrender), we should note the difference in process. The convert of the volitional type experiences a gradual progress of maturational growth as the psychologist sees it

(Fergeson, 1967:14), or of socialization as the anthropologist understands it (Loewen, 1969:1), whereas the experience of the self-surrender type is almost entirely unconscious or subliminal.

It is interesting to note that the gradual process of conversion is likely to occur in second-, third-, and fourth-generation Christians, rather than in non-Christian contexts, as I will show later. This may happen so gradually that the one being socialized into Christian faith recognizes very few, if any, peak experiences; he may rather go through a series of transitional stages of maturation which are so gradual, as the case story of the weaver illustrates, that the convert himself fails to notice them. Thus Evangelist Billy Graham speaks of "many forms of conversion" of which no two are exactly alike. Graham (1967:279) also points out that his wife, for example, cannot remember the exact time when she became a Christian, but she knows and demonstrates that she is one now. Loewen's comments are noteworthy in this connection:

> This "successive-stages" approach certainly also has experiential validity for "Christian socialization." Most people looking back upon their Christian development can point to a number of stages in which their commitment was deepened and extended. Even conversion-preaching groups find that a certain percentage of their membership cannot point to a definite time and a definite place of conversion, but rather to a series of affirmations matching their emotional and intellectual maturation (1969:4).

Professor Theodor Haarbeck (1846-1923), eminent Bible teacher and theologian of the early fellowship movement (Gemeinschaftsbewegung) in Germany, dealt with the same question during a time of great revival in his nominally-

Christian, state church. Haarbeck says that conversion can happen suddenly, in successive stages, and in gradual progression. "Ordinary, pious people," Haarbeck observes (1922:143), "can gradually grow into a wealth of the Christian salvation experience without associating the experience itself with radical conversion. They know that they are converted but they do not know when they were converted."

Whatever the nature and duration of these experiences might be that change a person's value system and lifestyle, the normal rule is that there is an initial experience and a later validating crisis, as the renowned Christian anthropologist and linguist Dr. Jacob A. Loewen points out (1969:5). The rather interesting observation is that there seems to be a correlation between type A in the Christian context and type C in a totally non-Christian context. In both cases the validating crisis came at the time when the person was baptized, thereby sealing his covenant relationship with God and publicly joining the community of believers, which is the church of Jesus Christ.

Conversion in Relation to Evangelism

On the basis of the above observations on empirical and experiential conversion data, it appears that the three basic types of conversion may take a variety of forms: (a) The gradual, process or volitional type; (b) the self-surrender or sudden climactic type; and (c) the stage or peak-experience type, which may involve a series of decisions in a long process.

Conversion Forms and Evangelism Stages

As we have shown in the analysis of the empirical and experiential conversion concepts above, each of the three

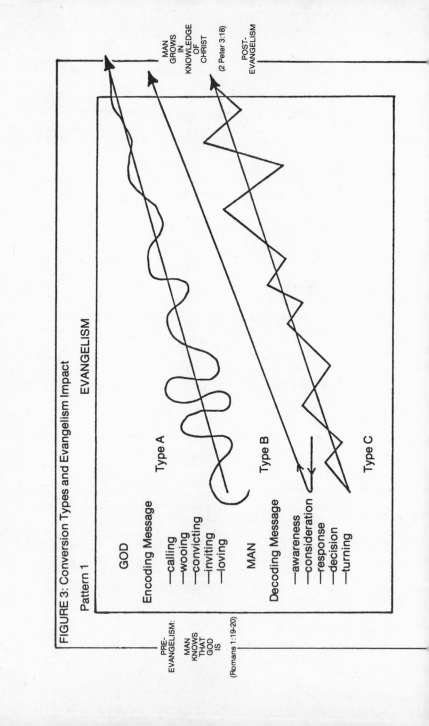

FIGURE 3: Conversion Types and Evangelism Impact

Pattern 1   EVANGELISM

PRE-
EVANGELISM:
MAN
KNOWS
THAT
GOD
IS

(Romans 1:19-20)

GOD

Encoding Message
—calling
—wooing
—convicting
—inviting
—loving

MAN

Decoding Message
—awareness
—consideration
—response
—decision
—turning

Type A

Type B

Type C

MAN
GROWS
IN
KNOWLEDGE
OF
CHRIST
(2 Peter 3:18)

POST-
EVANGELISM

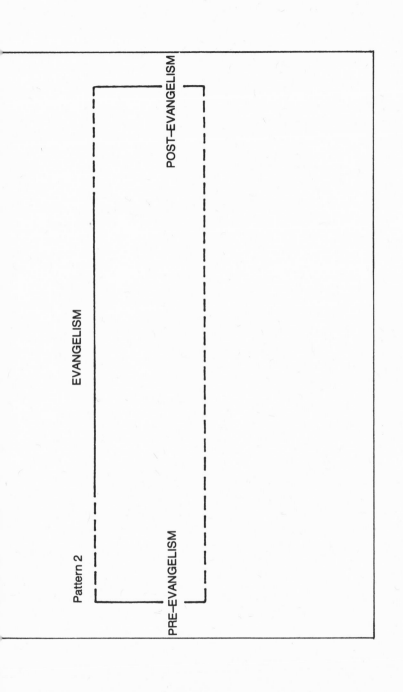

Pattern 2

EVANGELISM

PRE-EVANGELISM

POST-EVANGELISM

basic types—A, B, and C—may take a variety of forms. Figure 3 is an attempt to schematize these basic experiences, all indicating an initial as well as a "terminal point," without forcing the experience itself to terminate. Conversion leads to discipleship in the believers' church, and discipleship is an ongoing process of growth, maturation, internalization of Christian values, and sanctification. Such growth leads one into a dynamic relationship with other people. But this new life must have a beginning, a beginning in the decision to follow Jesus Christ as Savior from sin and Lord of life. Robert Raines has put it well when he says:

> We start in the direction of Christian discipleship when we say "yes" to Christ. One does not become a Christian overnight, but he may make the first step overnight or in a moment of decision . . . there can be no growth unless and until there is a decision; one can make no progress along the road until one decides to take the road. As someone has written: "So many in our churches are busily continuing something they never anywhere decisively began." One does not become a Christian by receiving secondhand the faith of his fathers; no one becomes a Christian *in absentia*, or in his sleep; one *decides* to follow Christ (Raines, 1961:42).

But even prior to the decision to follow Christ, there is often an initial point of awareness of an existing need. This felt need may already exist in a pre-evangelism time or it may be brought about through evangelism. What this says is that the entire conversion process, from the initial point of need-awareness to the point when responsible discipleship under Christ's lordship in the believers' church at the post-evangelism stage begins, is, indeed, a complex one. It reflects a manifold work of God; it requires a manifold ministry from His servants; it necessitates a manifold response from those who receive ministry (Oliver, 1975:1).

The Three Types and Two Patterns

The diagram (Figure 3 on pages 76 and 77) reflects man's turning around and moving positively toward God. Type A illustrates the conscious, voluntary, gradual rather uneventful move, though not totally without minor ups and downs in life, until the Holy Spirit completes the new birth and the life of sanctification sets in. Type B is the sudden crisis experience where a person (or a group of persons) makes a sudden change in life and relationships. For Type C conversion is a long process, yet it occurs in peaks or a series of crises, some more important than others, as Kraft points out. The more powerful the experience, the greater is the change in the person's life. In every type there are many factors—such as emotional concomitants of the individual or group, peer pressure or obstruction, the mental decoding of the gospel message on the part of the hearer, the cultural milieu, and the newness or unexpectedness of the person's whole experience. All these factors—and many more—play a considerable role in the total conversion experience (cf. Kraft, 1973b:383-384).

It should also be noted, as Pattern 2 of the diagram attempts to show, that it cannot always be determined when the time of pre-evangelism ends and that of evangelism sets in, or where evangelism terminates and post-evangelism (nurture) begins. It is important to note that the Christian experience must be ongoing, even in the post-evangelism (nurture) stage beyond the point of conversion, lest the person or group rely on "cheap grace" without further growth and manifestation of the new life in Christ that is demonstrated in the covenant relationship of the people of God. The point of conversion, however, can be defined as that of encounter where divine justification and human faith meet, the point at which reconciliation takes place, the point at which one decides to follow Christ. Henceforth, the person is a new creature, a child of God.

Summary

We have classified the conversion types discussed above as Type A, Type B, and Type C. The first two emerge from the Jamesian definition which enhances our total understanding of religious experience from a psychological perspective, regardless of whether or not it is rooted in biblical teaching. The third type is based on a later study by the Jewish scholar Abraham Maslow. On the basis of these empirical studies we have delineated the three types of conversion experience. The volitional type, or the conscious, voluntary regenerative change takes place in a person who eventually falls back on the "larger Power," which we recognize as the Holy Spirit, who completes the work of the new birth in that person. The self-surrender type is the sudden, instantaneous, cataclysmic experience which changes a person from the old to the new life in Christ. Finally, the peak-experience type may consist of a series of climactic experiences which bring a person to the point of submission to Christ and the realization that life is, indeed, worth living.

In terms of the processes involved, Type A is diagrammed as a gradual curve, representing a decision for Christ somewhat like the wake of a boat created by the boat's gradual turn and its subsequent move in the opposite direction. The course toward the harbor, however uneventful, may have slight curves in it. Type B is drawn as a line going in one direction, making a sudden turnabout, henceforth moving in the opposite direction. It is, perhaps, best illustrated by the course of the prodigal son who moves away from his father, but then suddenly changes his course, going back toward his father. Type C is seen as a line in open life, having no direction until an awareness is being created that there is more to life than one has experienced or is aware of until that moment. At this time a meandering begins, leading from one peak experience to another until the final decision, that of following Christ, has been reached. Here the soul comes to rest because it has found peace and rest in God.

How this process takes place in theological perspective is best seen in terms of reconciliation of a sinful and estranged person resulting in a new relationship at conversion. To that I must now turn.

Chapter 5

Reconciliation and Relationship: A Theological Concern

Jesus Christ rehabilitated the human race; He put it back to where God designed it to be.

—*Oswald Chambers*, 1945

The theologian approaches the subject of conversion from a theocentric perspective and insists that, in order to be rightly understood, man must be seen "in the light of God's revelation of Himself in Christ"; the cultural anthropologist approaches the subject of conversion from an anthropocentric perspective, insisting that man is the beginning, the center, and the end of his subject (Sharpe, 1969:230).

I am here concerned with the theological question of conversion, but not without giving consideration to ethnological principles at work. I shall, however, omit such controversial issues as divine grace and human freedom, prevenient or infused grace and human-divine cooperation, election and predestination—all issues which Catholic and Protestant theologians alike have debated about for centuries and continue doing so in our day (cf. Bloesch, 1968:78 f.). My concern here is to deal more with the existential than with the theoretical aspects of conversion. It is imperative to bear in mind that God deals with people at the level of their existence; within their own culture God provides points of contact for reconciliation and conversion.

Case Story: How the Sawi People Were Reconciled

In a culture where trickery and treachery are idealized as highest values, traitors and torturers are venerated as the greatest heroes. So it was with the Sawi people of Dutch New Guinea or Irian Jaya when Don and Carol Richardson came to live among them in 1962 (1974:185 ff.).°

There was neither token nor gift big enough, neither treaty nor pact binding enough, to authenticate a peace agreement between the warring Kamur and Haenam villages, save one—the peace child.

"Tomorrow we are going to sprinkle cool water on each other!" said the leading men of both warring factions to Richardson one late evening. What they meant was that they were going to make peace and be reconciled. Despite the disbelief on the part of the missionary, the men meant what they said. They were about to make peace at the sacrifice of two children—a peace child from each group.

Kaiyo of Kamur had—despite pleading and anguish of his wife—taken his only son, the six-month-old Biakadon. Holding him close to his chest one last time, he headed toward the people of Haenam. As he stood there, facing the tense crowd of children, women, and the warring men, he saw the man he had chosen to bear his name, and called, "Mahor!"

°Don Richardson's book, *Peace Child*, is a classic in recent mission literature. His concept of "redemptive analogy" is a significant contribution to the ethnotheological understanding of Christian conversion. The far-reaching effects of multi-personal conversion in Irian Jaya (the setting for *Peace Child*) are recorded in *The Lords of the Earth*, 1977.

The man leaped forward and faced Kaiyo.

> "Mahor!" Kaiyo challenged. "Will you plead the words of
> Kamur among your people?"
> "Yes," Mahor responded, "I will plead the words of Kamur
> among my people!"
> "Then I give you my son and with him my name!" Kaiyo
> held forth little Biakadon, and Mahor received him gently into
> his arms.
> Mahor shouted, "*Eehaa!* "It is enough! I will surely plead for
> peace between us!" . . .
> People now began calling Mahor by Kaiyo's name.
>   (Richardson, 1974:199)

As the intensity of the atmosphere increased, Mahaen of
Haenam held aloft one of his small sons named Mani, and
called,

> "Kaiyo! Will you plead the words of Haenam among your
> people?"
> "Yes!" cried Kaiyo, holding out his hands toward Mahaen.
> "Then I give you my son and with him my name!" As Kaiyo
> took the little boy, Mani, from Mahaen, a sudden cry of despair
> broke out from the back of the throng. Close relatives of the
> child had just realized what was happening (Richardson,
> 1974:200).

As the two babies, Biakadon and Mani, were being
decorated by their respective adopted villages for an authentic peace celebration, the missionary inquired about the
meaning of all this. A young man explained, "Tuan [white
man], you've been urging us to make peace—don't you
know it's impossible to have peace without a *peace child?*"
(Richardson, 1974:201).

This was the key the Richardsons had been praying for.

As the ancestors of the Sawi people had passed down the

words of a peace child to bring about peace and reconciliation between two warring peoples, so the ancestors of the
missionaries had passed down a story of a Peace Child—
God's Son—to make peace not only between the warring
villages of the Sawi, but also of the Sawi with their *Myao
Kodon*, the God of heaven and earth.

This "redemptive analogy from their own culture"
(Richardson, 1974:221) eventually led to permanent and
spiritual reconciliation and relationship of the Sawi people.

The Meaning and Function of Reconciliation

According to Paul, reconciliation of the holy, saving God
with sinful, separated humanity is Christ's offer to all people
(Romans 1:16; Ephesians 2:13-16). Reconciliation means the
removal of an existing barrier between two parties at enmity
or war. In the context of this study, the barrier is sin (see
Chapter 2) in its manifold forms and functions. Sin not only
alienates and bars persons from God their Maker, but also
from others, their brothers and sisters. Sin also separates and
fences off one ethnic group from another (Ephesians 2:11-
22).

In Christ, the authentic Peace Child, God not only justifies the individual in isolation, He also reconciles the estranged to Himself and to others in relationships.

What has really taken place in the transaction on the cross
is that God has provisionally forgiven the sin of the sinner.
He has pardoned his guilt; He has withdrawn the punitive
verdict.

God did all this because Christ, the Mediator, was willing
to have the Lord God cause "the iniquity of us all to fall on
Him" (Isaiah 53:6, NASB). The prophet Isaiah has pro-
phetically put into words what the Lord God has historically
actualized through Christ (Chapter 53):

5. He was pierced through for our transgressions,
    He was crushed for our iniquities;
    The chastening for our well-being fell upon Him,
    And by His scourging we are healed.
11. As a result of the anguish of His soul,
    He will see it and be satisfied;
    By His knowledge the Righteous One,
    My servant, will justify the many,
    As He will bear their iniquities (NASB).

Every forgiven sinner is a justified saint who by faith
trusts in the Lord for salvation and redemption, present and
future. The Baroque poet Friedrich Hiller (1699-1769),
whose songs the believers' church still likes to sing, expressed it this way in a song:

> Guilt an punishment are cancelled;
> God is merciful to me.
> I may claim this word of pardon,
> May rejoice by faith: "I'm free!"
> Praise the Lord, my soul, do praise Him
> For the great Redeemer's love.
> All His mandates now are gracious,
> Pointing to His courts above.
>
> My account is closed forever;
> Jesus Christ has paid it all.
> He did shed His blood to cover,
> He delivered me from fall.
> Not one penny stands against me,
> Many millions did He pay.
> Oh my Lord, what could have happened,
> If you had not set me free?
> (*Gesangbuch*, 1955:220, translation mine.)

"The power of forgiveness, both divine and human," said
Israeli Peace Activist Joseph Abileah in a chapel talk at

Fresno Pacific College, "has never been tested to its limits." This applies to God's forgiveness of human guilt as well as to forgiveness in interhuman and international relations. Both have profound bearing on the meaning and functions of reconciliation.

God has given the message of reconciliation and forgiveness to His servants. They are to proclaim that message both within, across, and above cultural boundaries. Thus Paul could say: "We are ambassadors for Christ . . . be reconciled to God" (2 Corinthians 5:20, RSV). The desired response to this appeal is, in fact, a conversion experience, a turning in repentance to God while God turns in forgiveness to the repentant one.

The meeting point is that of reconciliation, the point when the person—regardless of his religious or cultural status—becomes a *new person* in Christ. This does not mean that he becomes *neos*, or new in point of time, but *kairos*, or new in point of quality. Thus when a person is converted to God, it does not mean that Christ Jesus "makes all Jews into Gentiles or all Gentiles into Jews; He produces a new kind of person out of both, although they remain Gentiles and Jews" (Barclay, 1959:136).

What is significant in terms of individual or personal conversion is that both Jew and Gentile are new people in Christ, comprising the one new covenant people of God (2 Corinthians 5:17; 1 Peter 2:9-10). Jesus has removed the barriers between God and humanity and the fences between different peoples. "He abolished all religion that is founded on rules and regulations, and brought to man a religion whose foundation is love" (Barclay, 1959:135).

Commenting on Ephesians 2:16, the renowned Bible scholar, William Barclay, explains the matter of reconciliation this way:

The word that Paul uses (*apokatallassein*) is the word which
is used of bringing together friends who have been estranged.
The work of Jesus is to show all men that God is their friend,
that they must be friends with each other. *Reconciliation with
God involves and necessitates reconciliation with man*
(1959:136-37, italics mine).

The Meaning of Relationship

Professor Barclay's comments have already indicated the
direction in which reconciliation with God leads, namely to
reconciliation within the human race. This finds expression
in new relationships in a twofold dimension: between
persons and God and among people. The new persons and
peoples in Christ are now disciples under the lordship of
Jesus expressing their newfound religion not only creedally,
but also by identification with a new people of God in a relational theology of love to God and humanity. The Apostle
John explains the matter thus: "And this commandment we
have from him, that he who loves God should love his
brother also" (1 John 4:21).

Intrinsic Elements

We have already commented on the importance of community and fellowship of the visible believers' church. But
here we must expand on that concept in the context of relationship. Bishop Lesslie Newbigin of Madras has led us to
several significant insights in his book, *The Finality of Christ*
(1969:92-98). Newbigin points out that the total conversion
experience has from its very beginning three intrinsic elements. In the first place, there is the subjective, inward religious experience of turning heart and mind to God. Such
turning establishes the vertical relationship with the God-
head. Second, there is, what Newbigin terms the actual

commitment to a community of believers,' which is a visible
fellowship in society. This community constitutes the
Gemeinde der Gläubigen, the believers' church or the brotherhood-church, as the Anabaptists of the sixteenth century
conceived of it (Friedmann, 1973:81). This community,
furthermore, gives dynamic expression to the vertical
covenant relationship of the converted with their God on the
one hand and to the horizontal relationship with the people
of God on the other. That means a new ethic.

The Role of Believer's Baptism

The act by which the converts visibly and symbolically affirm their covenant and form the community is believer's
baptism, called "the covenant of a good conscience with
God" (1 Peter 3:21). The significance of the act of baptism
for the new convert, as Friedmann has pointed out, can
hardly be overestimated (Friedmann, 1973:135-36).

1. Baptism is an external, visible demonstration of the
internal, spiritual experience, known as the new birth (Titus
3:7; Acts 2:38). That is why we speak of believer's baptism,
rather than adult baptism.

2. Believer's baptism is also a sign of identification of the
new converts with other believers; it is the act of incorporation of the spiritually newborn children of God with others
already a part of the family of God.

3. Furthermore, baptism is a dramatic demonstration of
dying to the old way of life—by being buried with Christ in
the water grave—and of rising to the new way of life—by
being raised out of the water grave—that the young Christian henceforth "walk in newness of life" (Romans 6:3-11).
Elsewhere, this is expressed as an act of "putting off the old
nature which belongs to the former manner of life of corrup-
tion and deceit, and putting on the new nature created after

the likeness of God in righteousness and holiness" (Ephesians 4:22-24).

4. Baptism may also be described as an act of obedience by the church who conforms to the biblical mandate to make disciples (Matthew 28:16-20), as well as an act of obedience by the believing convert who receives it (cf. Acts 8:12; 35-39; 9:17-18; 10:44-48).

5. As already indicated, baptism is the new Christian's way of saying farewell to the old life and of identifying with the community of believers (Acts 2:40-47). Without the act of identification and incorporation, the young convert's life remains in a kind of "no-man's-land." It no longer belongs to the Fourth World, but neither does it assume responsibility in the body of Christ.

6. Finally, believer's baptism implies an acceptance of, and a commitment to, a new pattern of conduct which is demonstrative of the spiritual change brought about in conversion. This changed pattern of conduct (Newbigin, 1969:98) is what the Anabaptists called "the new and redemptive way" (Klassen, 1973:17), which is expressed in sundry horizontal dimensions.

How far this change is evidenced in the conversion of young people who grow up in Christian homes is difficult to ascertain. In many instances such children have experienced a preventative grace by not noticeably living in sins, although they are sinners by nature. The change is less obvious in children than in adult converts, particularly in the realms of the ethical.

The Function of Relationship

The late E. Stanley Jones (1884-1973) quotes a psychiatrist as saying, "There are three basic attitudes we can take toward others—to move away from them, to move against them, to move towards them." Jones goes on to say that the first two attitudes "are cancelled in conversion" and that the converts give up their attitudes of escapism and antagonism and "begin to move toward others—in love" (1959:132). Thus the path of the new converts always leads to fellow believers in the brotherhood-church. Here they receive and give by sharing. But their path also leads them back to the people in the Fourth World. There they serve and witness to God's mercy, grace, and love by caring—until the Lord returns.

Relational Theology in Action

In "The Company of the Committed," as Elton True-blood has so aptly put it in a book title (1961), the new converts never walk their road alone. Together with other covenant people of God, they flesh out a relational theology that is neither egocentric nor ethnocentric, but Christocentric and other-centered. A new life under Christ's lordship is filled with Christian love in discipleship. Christians corporately experience joy and sorrow, blessing and grief, good and bad, healing and sickness, defeat and victory. The Anabaptists' thesis that man comes to God together with his brother (Friedmann, 1973:81) finds its indisputable validation in a functional relationship. The community of believers is a community of mutual care and encouragement, whether such encouragement be needed in a time of new adventure or in a time of shame and failure.

Leslie E. Mark an evangelical churchman from Guadalajara, Mexico, asks the probing question whether American Evangelicalism bases its conversion concept on "cheap grace." The real problem in it all, contends Mark (1975:2), "is the belief that conversion is all that is necessary for receiving all the benefits of salvation." Mark's observation that the fruits of the conversion experience must be lived out in a covenant relationship endorses what I want to say on this matter and merits to be quoted at length. He describes the unifying and ethically visible factors operative in the people of God in covenant in these terms:

> It is not enough to be individually reconciled and to submit to God's will and moral law in a vacuum. The covenant provides the prerogatives, the premises, and the conditions of being a people of God. These are summarized negatively in the Ten Commandments and positively in the Sermon on the Mount. These are entirely relational. Any religious ceremonies which automatically bring grace are absent.
>
> How then, does one become a member of this people? He does so by a responsible decision to abandon all his sin, to submit himself to the plain teachings of Holy Scriptures in union with others of the same persuasion. This is what it means to believe in Christ and to love God (John 14:15, 21; 15:10; 1 John 5:3).
>
> This is not accomplished alone and instantaneously ordinarily. The revealing of sins is a process which takes place in the progressive light of learned Scripture. No one can surrender the sins today which are not revealed until tomorrow. Repentance and renewal continues. Neither is this accomplished alone. Christianity is relational and social, and although isolated conversions have occurred, the entire concept is that of union and progress in a covenant relationship with others for mutual admonition, discipline, help, and instruction. The competitive individualism of Protestantism is noticeably absent from the biblical idea of the people of God. Thus, we see that we are a people of God. Thus, we see that we are a people bound together under a relational, encouraging, behavioral covenant
>
> (Mark, 1975:3).

Reconciliation Demonstrated

In such relational theology as described by Mark, conversion is interpreted as being as dynamic as the life of disciple-

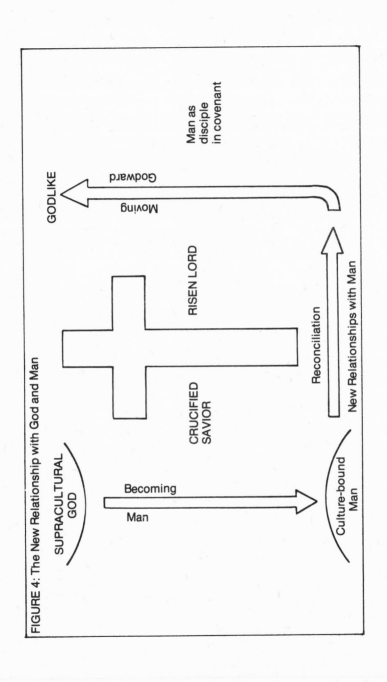

FIGURE 4: The New Relationship with God and Man

SUPRACULTURAL GOD

Becoming Man

Culture-bound Man

CRUCIFIED SAVIOR

RISEN LORD

Reconciliation

New Relationships with Man

GODLIKE

Moving Godward

Man as disciple in covenant

ship itself. God has taken the initiative by coming to humanity in His own Son. He gave His Peace Child, the Prince of Peace, to reconcile persons to Himself. In the conciliatory process, God is becoming human in order that humankind might become more like God. Christ's death on the cross and His resurrection from the grave demonstrate this fact, as I have shown above. By His death the sinner is reconciled and justified; by His resurrection he receives new life. With the event of justification commences reconciliation; with the event of reconciliation begins the life of sanctification in a new relationship. A new power has taken control and a new direction has set in. "The process can be described as the reverse process of the Incarnation," says William Keeney (1973-1974:6). We may still suffer from the habits of the old nature, but the central force and direction of movement are according to the new nature (Figure 4, page 93).

To describe the illustration, I can do no better than borrow the following words from Keeney:

> Man learns to know God and communicates a knowledge of God really as he practices his relationship to man. Jesus incarnated the meaning of divine manhood when he deliberately chose to take the way of the suffering Servant. He demonstrated the way of suffering love which bore the evils of man's sin without repaying it in kind. He showed us the power of "powerlessness," the transformation of evil into good by the power of God. The cross stands as the supreme symbol of this love and the resurrection confirms its power. He calls us to take up the cross and follow Him (1973-1974:6).

Life for the new converts becomes most meaningful when responsibilities are reciprocal. Although conversion, reconciliation, and forgiveness of sins have been personally experienced and appropriated, they never remain individualistic in their fruition. In fact, they mark "the end of individualism and the entry into fellowship" (Barclay, 1972:71). In this new "fellowship of forgiven sinners," as Dr. Myron Augsburger (1964:61) has put it, the converts build new relationships and actively demonstrate their discipleship under Christ's lordship. In this fellowship, they corporately worship, pray, fast, and study God's Word; here they remember and proclaim the Lord's redemptive work; here they celebrate around the communion table their Lord's death, resurrection, and coming again; here they listen to the prophets and teachers in their midst; here they experience the call of the apostolate and of sentness into the Fourth World from whence they themselves have come; here they learn to obey when the Holy Spirit bids them to set apart a "Barnabas" and a "Saul," a "Stephen" and a "Philip" for the special ministry to which the Lord has called them.

The function of relationship also touches the very core of human character in personal ethics, morals, lifestyles, and attitudes. The new converts learn what it means no longer to conform to the norms and standards of the world, regulated exclusively by the mores and pressures of the old sociocultural lifeway; they learn what it means to be transformed by the renewal of their minds and hearts; they learn to express this new way of life in harmony with the teachings of Jesus and His apostles, in new values and attitudes, in chastity and purity, in quality and beauty, in honesty and probity, in peaceful living with everyone, and in obedience to God.

Call to Responsibility

There is one other function of the new relationship that must be underscored as an integral part of the total conversion experience. It is the positive relationship of the new believer to unbelievers in eschatological perspective. Paul Löffler (1967b:257) reminds us that conversion "does not primarily refer to an affirmation of metaphysical beliefs, but to concrete obedience and a renewed relationship with one's neighbour." And what if that neighbor does not know the Son of God as his own ultimate Savior and Lord? What if that neighbor does not know the new life in Christ? Conversion to God is never a mere license to privileges; conversion is rather a call to responsibilities in the kingdom of God, present and future. Conversion is a key to witness and service opportunities in the non-Christian Fourth World and a case for involvement with others in view of their destiny.

It is true, the privileges of conversion are many, implying such benefits that come with "the deepest kind of personal cleansing, forgiveness, reconciliation, and renewal (Newbigin, 1969:112). But precisely therein lures the temptation for the new convert. Whenever he permits the accent to fall on the happy thought of "being saved" and on the rewarding privileges of being a member of a "saved community," the convert should beware of "cheap grace," as Dietrich Bonhöffer (1937:41) has reminded us. Cheap grace will not be sufficient in the final judgment.

Being converted and a member of the community of forgiven sinners places a tension of eschatological dimensions on the converts. Neither young nor old converts dare lose sight of the biblical view of humankind, their salvation, and their destiny. Conversion is no mere personal ticket to heaven. It is far more a divine call to sinful humanity to repent, be baptized, become a member of the believers' church, and thus build the kingdom of God. Men and women of the Fourth World become converted when believers participate collectively in the mighty acts of the redemptive work in Christ. Newbigin's comments are noteworthy:

Conversion will always be wrongly understood unless it is re-membered that the Church is the *pars pro toto* [a part for the whole]. God converts a man not only that he may be saved, but also that he may be the sign, earnest and instrument of God's total plan of salvation (1969:113).

Converts have broken their relationship with sin, but they must build relationships with sinners; they must become friends to sinners, not to sin. As they bear witness to the claims of Christ that He is, indeed, *the Friend* of sinners, the Savior of the world, and the Lord of life, they are extending a call to the unconverted everywhere to repent. "As a call," says Newbigin (1969:113), quoting Löffler, "it is uttered to all nations, as a potential it concerns the destiny of all men." This call into the kingdom is a dynamic process carried out in the power of the Holy Spirit until the King returns to gather all His subjects as one flock under one Shepherd.

Summary

When a person or a group of people is converted, a dual action is set in motion: God justifies, the converted believes; God forgives, the converted is forgiven. This results in recon-ciliation which produces new relationships. That means on the one hand that the barrier of sin which alienated people from God is removed; on the other hand it means that the fences and walls which before conversion separated people from each other are broken down. The divine *Peace Child*, to use the analogy of the case story again, has brought peace to both warring factions. The converts now have access to God, because they are forgiven; they also have fellowship with each other because all enmities that heretofore existed have now been overcome by love. Thus there is a vertical relationship with God and a horizontal relationship with others.

The converted have become partners with God by accepting God's offer of the new covenant through Christ. By the biblical ritual of believer's baptism, the converted have also become members of the visible body of Christ; they have identified themselves with the believers' church, which consists of other covenant people who, as themselves, have experienced conversion. This new relationship is corporately shared by common experiences like prayer, worship, Word study, witness, healing, fasting, and participation in the Lord's Supper. It is reciprocally shared by fellowship, exhortation, encouragement, and mutual care for the glorification of God through the whole body.

But the new relationship is also shared with unbelievers who are still in the Fourth World. This type of sharing is demonstrated by living in discipleship under the lordship of Christ and by giving witness to the love of God, so that all peoples might become reconciled to Him and live the abundant life under the kingship of Jesus Christ.

But how are lost men to be brought to Christ? Paul would lead us to believe, "Through the preaching of the gospel." That leads us to a further concern which we must now consider in the context of the mission of the church.

Chapter 6

Objectives in Opposites:
Missiological Concerns

The world just isn't big enough anymore for *anyone* to be left alone.   —*Don Richardson*, 1974

The question whether conversion is an individual or a group decision or both is a missiological one. Akin to this is the question of quality and quantity in the conversion experience. Is it possible, for example, that a group of people—a family, a clan, a tribe, a homogeneous unit in society, or an entire social subsystem—can make as valid a decision and arrive at as high a degree of commitment to the saviorhood and lordship of Jesus Christ as one individual? Or is conversion always an individual matter as Western Christians seem to think? Does quantity in conversion of a whole *ethne*, a people, impair quality? An unqualified positive or negative answer to these questions would hardly be justified, let alone satisfactory. A qualifying answer, however, raises still another question, namely the question of our understanding of individualism and community and their relationship to conversion within individualistic and communal societies.

Case Story: The Multi-Personal Conversion
of Papua Tribes

Missionary Christian Keysser (1877-1961) of New Guinea began to proclaim a message of reconciliation and peace to the Papua who were constantly at war with kin tribes. Anutu, said Keysser to his host people, is a God of peace who desires neither revenge nor bloodshed.

Keysser was convinced that God wants to bring salvation to *panta ta ethne*, to all and whole peoples, not only individuals. Therefore, he was guided by the principle of multipersonal conversion. After preaching the gospel for four years to the people of Mount Hagen, Keysser judged them to be ready to exchange paganism for the Christian way of life. Thus he called a great assembly at the airport and, according to tribal custom, provided a feast for the 18,000 assembled. They grouped themselves by tribes round a high pulpit and discussed the implication of a change from heathen practices to Christian discipleship.

The missionary mounted the pulpit, prayed, and delivered the following message (Vicedom, 1962):

"Friends, today you have come to take part in a great festival. No one has compelled you. You have come of your own free will, because God has called you. That is very fine, and we are glad of it. Today you wish to give up your heathen ways, and to accept Christianity. No one has compelled you to do this either. You have heard God's Word, and now you cannot get free from God. That is why you have decided to take this step. Now it may be that there are many here who in their hearts are not ready to take this step. They are here only because they would feel ashamed, if they stayed away. Perhaps, while they are here, they will say 'Yes,' and then, when they get back home, will go on with their old ways. God is not pleased with such conduct. What you promise here you must carry out. So I pray you—do not mock God. You cannot hide your hearts from

God. He sees everything that you are doing today. God hears every word you say. God knows your thoughts. If you are not serious in your intentions, go back home. But if you really wish to come to God—do the work!"

All the people listened intently. The tribes were represented by their chiefs. One by one the chiefs approached the pulpit, holding small pieces of wood in their hands. Now an indigenous ceremony of conversion followed, rich in symbolism and meaning, as each chief addressed his people in approximately the following manner.

"See, my people; here I have in my hand a piece of wood. Its name is war. You know how we used to fight with one another. No one could go anywhere without fear. We could not sleep at night for pricking up our ears at every sound. Since the Word of God came to us, peace has returned. Now for the first time we know how pleasant life can be. Now what is your choice? Shall we go back to fighting as we used to do, or shall we continue to live in peace?" The people answered: "We choose peace. We promise never to go to war again." The chief continued, "See now, as I throw away this piece of wood, so we cast war away. From henceforth everyone among us shall live in safety. We will not kill any more!" The people responded, "We will not kill any more."

The chief resumed, "Here I have a stick called sorcery. We used to be even more afraid of sorcery than we were of war. If anyone was ill, he at once said to himself, 'I am bewitched.' If any misfortune happened, it was the sorcerer who had been at work. If our crops did not prosper, we attributed it to sorcery. Sorcery is the mother of fear. God's Word has driven out sorcery. No one speaks about it any more. When we are ill, God heals us by means of medicines. Now what is your choice? Shall we keep sorcery, or shall we decide not to put up with it any longer?" The people replied: "We have learned to pray. Never again will we have anything to do with sorcery." The chief: "See now, as I throw this piece of wood away—away with sorcery! Henceforth sorcery shall not be practiced here." The people: "Henceforth sorcery shall not be practiced here."

The chief: "My next piece of wood has to do with something that concerns women. You know what you did in old times when you had a baby. If you didn't like the baby, or if you were afraid of the work that it would cause, you did away with it. We men were often angry about this. To how many quarrels did it lead! God's Word tells us that it is God who gives us children. Now what is your choice? Do you intend to go on getting rid of the little ones as you used to do? Or are you prepared to bring them up as a gift from God?" The women: "We will obey God. We will bring up the children and not get rid of them." The chief: "See now, as I cast away this piece of wood, so we cast away child-murder from us. From now on no child shall be killed among us." The women: "From now on no child shall be killed among us."

In this way all the sins that were common among the people were worked through—theft, adultery, the worship of ancestors, and so on.

Following the ceremony of decision-making came the act of actual commitment to God. The chiefs held new, clean, and empty nets before their people, comparing these nets to empty hearts. "You have shaken out all your sins. Nothing evil is left in your hearts," the chiefs said. The people then expressed the desire that God should fill their empty hearts, lest the devil should come back and fill them again with evil things. The chiefs continued:

"See, God is here in the midst of you. God is here like this pole which stands firm and strong before you. No one can pull it up. No one can overturn it. It stands quite firm. In the same way God will never leave you. In this God you can completely trust. The man who wishes that God should enter into his empty heart must now commit himself to him."

Then the chiefs pointed to a pole standing immovably firm and to a bar which they held in their hands. "This pole stands for God," they said, "and the bar stands for us. If this bar is to be firm it must be tied to the pole."

"God and we belong to one another," the people affirmed. They expressed their desire to be bound firmly to God. Under the guidance of the missionary they chose the Word to tie them to God. Tying the bar to the pole, the missionary said, "God's Word is the rope. And so just as I bind the bar firmly to the pole with this rope, so I bind you firmly to God with God's own Word."

Once the tribes had verbally declared and symbolically demonstrated their will to be Christian and follow Christ, people began to be baptized—one by one, not in mass. "When it was finished, the people were satisfied that everything had been done in due and proper order" (Vicedom, 1962:123-128; cf. Keysser, 1949:32-48).

Individualism and Community in Conversion

Many critics of the church growth school of thought object to the movement because of its stress on quantity. It is, perhaps, not an unfair assumption to say that these critics base their position as much on their Western philosophy of individualism as on their theological conviction that their objective is "quality not quantity" (McQuilkin, 1973:12). We need to remember, however, that the philosophy of American individualism ensures neither quality nor quantity in Christian conversion. It can, moreover, be a serious deterrent to both.

Analysis and Explanation of Concepts

The concept of individualism as used in this study is neither to be equated with the selfhood of a person in society nor with personhood; nor should individualism be identified with the individuality of a person related to his natural and social environments. By individualism here is meant the philosophic concept of the eighteenth-century Enlightenment which holds that the individual is an independent entity in society who has the right to make certain claims on the social community in which he lives. The environment, in turn, has the right to make claims on the individual. But when either of the two dislikes the claim made by the other, then each has the right to refuse to comply, which leads to individual liberty without communal responsibility.

Emil Brunner (1889-1966) has called the philosophy of individualism "a 'Robinson Crusoe' affair, expressed in abstract terms." What Brunner means is that the philosophy of individualism is "an attempt to interpret the individual human being solely in the light of his own personality, and the society as the coalescence of such individuals" (1947:294).

This philosophy of individualism has invaded Christian thinking in the Western world in no small measure. In fact, Anglo-American Protestantism in general, and Fundamentalism in particular, perpetuate individualism even on the church level. Many well-meaning Christians consider it a highly valued spiritual heritage brought from Europe to America by Puritans and Pietists. This heritage was subsequently "indigenized" by revivalism, and thus it has become authentically incorporated into the American value system, in which it now occupies a high position.

Individualism has so profoundly shaped the American church concept that we find it difficult to conceive of the church as little more than a class of people consisting of "saved" or "converted" or "redeemed" individuals whose primary concern it is to retain their "individual rights," as though they had no communal and relational responsibility.

Such philosophy is a contradiction in terms. Just as the

physical world does not exist of, nor can it be explained by, isolated atoms, so society cannot exist of individuals in isolation. If we apply this principle to the church of believers as the body of Christ, which exists as a real, visible, sociological entity in the larger society, then we may say that the individual as such does not and cannot exist at all, save in responsible relationships, and that the very concept of the believing individual implies and includes that of the believing community (cf. Brunner, 1947:294-95).

This is not to say, however, as D. T. Niles (1962:106) seems to indicate, that salvation occurs whenever a person participates in God's work or in the "saving ministry of Jesus." The essence of conversion as it relates to the individual as well as to the community has been more perceptively delineated by the late missionary statesman, R. Kenneth Strachan (1910-1964). While speaking on personal conversion and commitment to Jesus Christ, Strachan says in his book, *The Inescapable Calling:*

> In dealing with the subject of individual salvation it is necessary to keep in mind that no man lives to himself, that growth and fellowship and service and witness are necessarily experienced in relationship to community and society. But to define salvation as participation in the collective ministry of the church, is to ignore that vast portion of Scripture in which salvation is defined in terms of the new birth and sonship or moral perfection and fellowship with God, and which sees the salvation of one single soul as of infinite value in the eyes of God (1968:35).

These observations lead us to conclude that conversion is personal, but not individualistic; it is experienced by individuals, but it affects the community; it is expressed in a vertical relationship, but not without horizontal dimensions. This principle becomes particularly significant for communal societies, as our case story in this chapter points out. But even in other societies it merits observation.

The Responsible Self in Relation to Community

The ethnotheological view of man in his dyadic and triadic relationships becomes helpful in understanding the fallacy of philosophic individualism and its barrier to Christian conversion and the believers' church.

Philosophic individualism and Christian conversion exclude each other. Thus individualism is anathema in conversion. Conversion, as defined earlier, always implies turning from some-*thing* to some-*One*, or from some-*one* to some-*One Else*. This concept is brought out rather forcefully by the American theologian, Richard Niebuhr (1894-1962), in his comprehensive essay on Christian moral philosophy, *The Responsible Self*. Like Emil Brunner in his *Divine Imperative* (1947), Niebuhr stresses the "social character of all human life" and states that the human person as "the self-making agent is not a lonely self" (1963:69). As a rational being, the human person is the knower and exists in the presence of ideas; as a moral being, he is the law-acknowledger and lives in the presence of mores and laws. But first and foremost, each person is a social self who not only knows self "in relation to other selves but exists as self only in that relation" (Niebuhr, 1963:71).

Both Brunner and Niebuhr make reference to Martin Buber's (1878-1965) existential reflections on the "I-It" and "I-Thou" relationships. To this two-dimensional natural/theological emphasis, Niebuhr adds a useful third—the sociological "I-You" interaction. As we reflect on Niebuhr's concept of the triadic relationship—without following his thought to conclusion—several observations emerge.

1. The I-It reflects man's relationship to the natural,

which is impersonal, "purely objective or thing-like in nature" (Niebuhr, 1963:79). This is philosophic individualism's only recognized relationship, a mere thing-relationship.

2. The I-Thou reflects man's acknowledgment of and relationship to the metaphysical realm of the supracultural God, to whom the "I" is responsible. The power which alone can make the "I" responsible to the "Thou" is manifested by God Himself, asserts Brunner (1947:295). The I-Thou or human-divine encounter takes place in the experience of Christian conversion. But this encounter does not happen in isolation; it happens in relationship to a third from which the I-Thou relationship is distinguished, yet to whom it responds.

3. The third dimension just referred to is the I-You relationship, the sociological companion(s) of the "I." By this we confirm the premise that God converts people always in the context of their social and cultural environment. When one is converted, the impact is so profound that the natural, the sociocultural, and the spiritual realms are all significantly affected.

The above delineations help us underscore the fact that Christian conversion is as much relational as it is personal. The "I" experiences personal salvation in a faith commitment to the "Thou"; therein lies the sonship for the person "I." Personal faith in the atoning death of Christ on the cross goes hand in hand with the new birth which the Holy Spirit performs in each person. Personal conversion, however, touches every relationship, whether it be natural, human, or divine.

In the work of creation, God acted as a holy "We" when He said, "Let *Us* make man in *Our* image, according to *Our* likeness; and let *them* rule over ... all the earth" (the natural "It," Genesis 1:26, NASB). Thus the God of crea-

tion, the divine "Thou," created man, the social "I-You,"
not in isolation, but in a sociological man-woman community. Suzanne De Dietrich's observation is noteworthy
when she says:

> The Trinitarian God is a fellowship of love and can only be
> reflected on the human plane in a living relationship. Only a
> human "we" can reflect something of the divine "Us"
> (1958:22).

One of the evangelical missiologists' chief concerns is that
God wants all people everywhere to be converted. Akin to
this is the conviction that God does not only want isolated individuals; He desires the gospel of the kingdom to be
presented to *ta ethne* (the peoples), the entire sociocultural
units or groups of people, such as families, tribes, and clans,
that they may respond to the divine invitation in a multi-
personal fashion.

A Lesson from Reformation History

One of the positive fruits of the Reformation was a
renewed understanding of salvation and conversion through
the divine-human encounter. Three major emphases became paramount, each relating directly to one of the
theological positions in vogue: the Catholic, the Protestant,
and the Anabaptist. The late Robert Friedmann (1891-1970)
has aptly described these positions thus:

> In Catholicism the believer is offered, as the only effective
> way to God and salvation, an intermediary, the institutional
> church with its reservoir of divine grace, and with its ordained
> priests who dispense the sacraments. In Protestantism this inter-
> mediary was radically done away with. Every individual
> believer stands in direct, unmediated relationship to his God,
> seeking and finding redemption by faith to the extent that he is

able to have such redeeming faith. In Anabaptism, finally, the answer is a combination of a vertical with a horizontal relationship. Here the thesis is accepted that man cannot come to God except together with his brother. In other words, the brother, the neighbor, constitutes an essential element of one's personal redemption. For the disciple there is no such thing as an isolated Christian in his lonely cell. To him brotherhood is not merely an ethical adjunct to Christian theological thinking but an integral condition for any genuine restoration of God's image in man (1973:80-81).

The analysis of the three historical positions may further be described in order as being "sacerdotal," "creedal," and "relational" in character. This can be illustrated by a diagram (Figure 5, page 110), which shows the concept of individualism and multi-personalism, and how man approaches God within the matrix of these concepts. Much like the New Testament church, the Anabaptists saw Christians always in corporate action, relationship, and responsibility.

Underscoring Highlights

Christian conversion, though it is personal, does not happen in isolation, but in the sociocultural context of the converts. Conversion always takes place within the experiencer's ethnic milieu. It does not happen in a state of independence of the individual, but in full dependence upon God's grace and mercy; it does not happen in an individualistic sense, but always in relational contexts. No one and nothing of the convert's environment remains unaffected, because of the fact that he has become a new person with changed attitudes to the "Thou," the "You," and the "It."

It must also be underscored that Christian conversion involves a power encounter, as Professor Alan Tippett

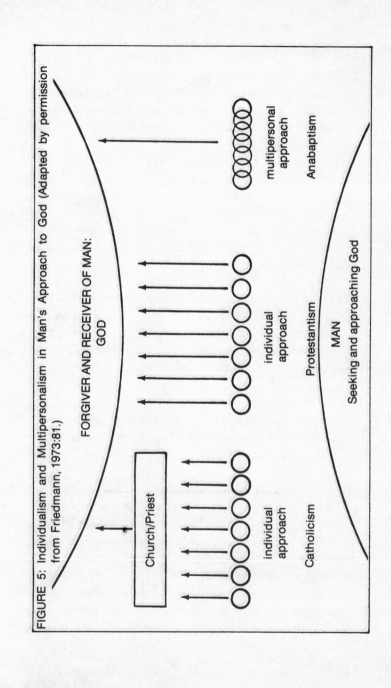

FIGURE 5: Individualism and Multipersonalism in Man's Approach to God (Adapted by permission from Friedmann, 1973:81.)

FORGIVER AND RECEIVER OF MAN: GOD

multipersonal approach

Anabaptism

individual approach

Protestantism

individual approach

Catholicism

Church/Priest

MAN

Seeking and approaching God

(1972:126) points out. This encounter is between light and darkness, grace and sin, good and evil, the highest and lowest value within a culture. It is, in the final analysis, an encounter between Christ and "demonic dynamism" (Tippett, 1972:127; Ephesians 6:11-12).

Salvation is in Christ alone and without knowledge of Him there can be no conversion. Christ must be universally presented in order that the manifestation of power can take place, for He alone is the "Lord of power," who demonstrates His *exousia,* His power with authority (Luke 10:19) over all other *dunamis,* the powers of the enemy (Tippett, 1972:142).

The encounter that takes place in conversion between the broken, divided, torn, multifaceted, inferior "I" and the whole, supreme, superior, supra-cultural "Thou" results in a covenant relationship, unknown before. That relationship, we have seen earlier, has both vertical and horizontal dimensions, as the New Testament leads us to understand. Whether people enter that relationship one by one or in groups of sociocultural units does not alter the principle of relationship and dependency. That remains the same. The existential expression of that principle is best seen in discipleship under Christ's lordship.

Guilt Culture and Shame Culture

Missiology is not only concerned that the messenger of the reconciliatory message has an adequate concept of humanity and its relational interdependence; it is equally concerned that the cross-cultural communicator of the gospel be thoroughly versed in the nature and function of the culture in which he seeks to bring the greatest possible quantity of people to the best possible quality of discipleship. He must know, for example, how people of a guilt cul-

ture respond differently to his message than people in a
shame culture. He should also understand the difference
between what may be called "ontologic" or "existential
guilt", which is normal, because it is based on real sin, and
"neurotic guilt," which may be caused by depressive feelings rather than by sin (Leon, 1975:1155).

God appeals to persons by the Holy Spirit, His special
Agent. Persons respond to that appeal by virtue of their
Creator-likeness. For the human spirit, says Dr. Myron
Augsburger (1970:90) is "the expression of the *Imago Dei*."
Even "in the worst of man," says the Argentinian
psychologist-theologian Jorge A. Leon, "there is the *image
of God*, asking for completion" (Leon, 1975:1159). The
German poet Johann Scheffler (1624-1677) expressed the
Creator-creature relationship this way:

> Lord, Thine image Thou has lent me
> In Thy never fading love;
> I was fallen, Thou wast sent me,
> My redemption from above.

> (*Worship Hymnal*, 1971:356.)

In this way, one is capable of experiencing authentic
conversion—a return to the Creator in repentance, a
renewal by the Redemptor in regeneration or re-creation.
The person becomes whole once again and free to interact
with his Maker; estrangement is ended, fragmentation has
ceased and the person returns from philosophical individualism and isolation to responsibility and reconciliation in
community with God and others (cf. Brunner, 1947:293 f.).

Thus Christian conversion always leads to relatedness and
the convert bears fruit in relational living. A newly

converted person becomes dependent on Christ; he becomes "Christonomous," to borrow a phrase from the
Tübingen theologian Peter Beyerhaus (1964:404 f.). When
this happens, the result is communion with God and interdependence (not independence) between fellow-believers.

From an ethnotheological perspective such experience
can easily be visualized to take place as readily in a Western
guilt culture as in an animistic fear culture or in a tribal
shame culture. In the one, conversion frees man from
existential guilt, in the other from haunting fear, and in still
another from defeating shame. Behind these phenomena,
however, is still the basic problem of human alienation from
God and from one another. Thus the difference may be less
in essence than in appearance. In every belief system and in
every cultural matrix, the convert will have to shift his
loyalty from whatever claims it now holds to the lordship of
Christ.

Anthropologists can help us at this juncture to understand
the difference between what we have termed a "shame culture" and a "guilt culture." The determining factors as to
whether one operates within one or the other are derived
from the value system of a given culture.

In *The Primal Vision* John V. Taylor (1963; German edition, 1965: 144), General Secretary of the Church Missionary
Society, speaks to this point. Like the Homeric man of
ancient times, says Taylor, so the African has for ages based
his value system more on a shame-culture than on a guilt-
culture. Although Taylor shows that such societies as the
Batutsi and the Lugbara of Ruanda are presently experiencing a transition, public opinion rather than a peaceful
conscience has, in the past, been considered the highest
value. The most unbearable experience a person can have in
such a society is to lose face by being laughed at or ridiculed

by others. Thus the greatest moral strength in a shame culture lies not in the fear and honor of God, but in receiving personal respect and honor from other humans.

In his analysis of a case study, Dr. Tippett constructs a schema of the value system of the Samoan way of life at the time when the Christian gospel was brought to the island. In an itemized continuum of five basic values he names *prestige* as the supreme positive value and *shame* at the very opposite pole as the extreme negative value. Whereas prestige is achieved through social and religious status, ostentation and generosity, demonstration of power, and proficiency in production, shame is derived "from failure in any of the above aspects or from slight or offense at any one of these points" (Tippett, 1971:151).

The prestige-shame poles of one axis are as important a value complex for the Samoans and countless other communal societies as the freedom-guilt poles of another axis form the basic value system for the Anglo-American Protestant culture.

The difference between the two systems has been analyzed and articulated by the renowned American anthropologist, Alfred Kroeber (1876-1960). He says that shame is felt, at least in part, with reference to others, and thus is externalized; guilt, which is derived from a sense of sin, is felt even in solitude with reference to self, and thus is internalized. Both the shame-bearing person and the guilt-ridden person, however, are subject to social control, disapproval, and correction. The difference is that the former can escape shame by leaving his immediate environment, whereas the latter is haunted by guilt even when he moves away from the place where guilt was incurred. Kroeber's observations on the distinction between a shame culture and a guilt culture are noteworthy:

Sin implies a disapproving conscience at work within oneself; shame, the knowledge that others disapprove; though shame can also be superadded to sense of sin—perhaps normally is so added. The distinction is not hard and fast; but it is polar.

Of late years, with conscious effort to define the ethos of cultures, a whole array of observers have made a similar finding on culture after culture. They encounter plenty of shame, but little or no sense of sin. Other people's opinions, their remarks, their ridicule or laughter, are what the average man, in most cultures, is sensitive to, is what deters him. This has been remarked equally for non-literate tribes and for literate nationalities. The Chinese are guided by "face-saving"; the Japanese lack the sense of "contrast of real and ideal" and "do not grapple with the problem of evil."

But the findings about the importance of shame as a social force are a bit too consistent. They leave little explicit sin sense to any culture but our own Occidental one; and within that largely to its Protestant portion, in fact outstandingly its Calvinistically influenced sector. It is true that sin and guilt, sin and trespass, sin and evil were rather imperfectly distinguished in Europe until the Reformation. It seems to have been this religious movement that internalized guilt and shame into sin, and reared conscience on a great pedestal (Kroeber, 1948:612).

It is imperative that every communicator of the gospel of the kingdom not only be familiar with the techniques of communication and the content of the message itself; he must also know the value system of his target culture in order to effect conversion to Jesus Christ as Lord of all life among the people he is seeking to change.

Conversion as Personal and Multipersonal Action

The psychologist, as we have seen, looks at the action and behavior of the individual. But the social anthropologist tends to look beyond the small world of his own culture in order to understand people as *people* within the framework of their total lifeway. The missiologist uses the tools of both and speaks of the conversion experience of a people as a "multi-individual decision," as Professor Alan Tippett of the School of World Mission has pointed out (1971:123-241).

An even more appropriate term to describe a group decision for Christ might be "multipersonal conversion," a concept which emerged as I discussed my conversion concerns with Tippett's colleague, Dr. Charles Kraft. Conversion is always personal, as I have shown earlier, but never individualistic. Thus, when an overwhelming majority within a sociological unit of people or a communal society makes a decision to accept Jesus Christ as Redeemer and First Chief or Lord, each person makes a personal commitment or covenant which touches every aspect of his own life as well as that of his fellowman. The Costa Rican theologian, Orlando E. Costas, has quite perceptively said:

> The concept of multi-individual decisions gives a sociological orientation to the experience of conversion because it affirms that conversion, which depends on a personal act of faith in Christ, can take place in a group setting, where all the members of a given group (family, clan, tribe, or mutual interest group) participate in a similar experience with Christ after considering it together and deciding to turn to Christ at the same time (1974:128).

It has been scientifically demonstrated by renowned missionaries of our time that the church of Jesus Christ around the world grows most rapidly by multipersonal conversions in group movements rather than by individual conversions in isolation (cf. Pickett, *et al.* 1936; McGavran, 1955a and 1955b; Tippett, 1971 and 1973, Vicedom, 1962:123-28).

It is significant that Gustav Warneck (1834-1910), the

father of Protestant missiology, wrote as early as 1874 about group conversion as the legitimate goal of mission. He supported his arguments by extensive biblical exegesis, a wealth of historical evidence, and case studies from missionary experience among the Chol people of Eastern India and the Batak of Sumatra (Warneck, 1874:41 ff.; 1902:243 ff.). Although Warneck always stressed the importance of single, personal conversion (1902:255), he maintained consistently over a period of four decades of fruitful missiological writing and teaching that the ultimate goal of preaching the gospel message must be to bring *panta ta ethne* (all ethnic groups or peoples to Christ (1902:257).

Just as the early missionaries of Acts baptized whole families and founded house churches, so the missionaries of today should aim at bringing whole families, groups, tribes, and peoples to Christ. "In essence the Christianization of entire peoples," says Warneck "is the same as the Christianization of families." Since the latter has been canonized (Acts 10:14; 11:14; 16:15, 33; 18:8; 1 Corinthians 1:16), there is no reason to believe that the former cannot be its theoretical as well as practical consequence. After all, the conversion of an ethnic people is the conversion of mere extended families (Warneck, 1902:260). He who seeks the conversion of individuals only engages in a spiritual "micro-enterprise," but he who helps entire families and peoples to submit to Christ as Savior from sin and Lord of life engages in a "macro-enterprise" for God (cf. Warneck, 1902:253; 257).

Quality in Quantity

The emphasis on *quantitative* group action in multipersonal conversion does not mean de-emphasis of *qualitative* personal conversion of individuals in that group. However, individualism, egocentrism, and ethnocentrism are characteristics of Western civilization, where family and group relationships are either broken up or only loosely observed. Small children are brought to nurseries or preschool "kiddy colleges"; old people are moved to isolated "senior citizens villages"; parents often separate or get a divorce, breaking up family relationships. All too often the European and American missionary's mentality is greatly influenced, perhaps even shaped, by such disintegrative conditions. He may think of them as acceptable, if not as normal. That is not to say that he condones or endorses them, but they have subconsciously become an integral part of the cultural milieu of which he is a product.

As the Western missionary moves out to share the gospel of Jesus Christ cross-culturally, he often fails to understand group cohesiveness operative as a communal principle and dominating social relationships in African, Asian, and some Latin American cultures. Here the missionary discovers even in totally non-Christian societies that "disloyalty to the group is a capital crime" (Warnshuis, 1973:9). At home the missionary observed disloyality as a way of life. This may affect his assessment of the new culture to which he has become an advocate of the gospel.

When the missionary suffers from "ethnomyopea" or sociocultural nearsightedness, he may not only fail to understand the value of group function, he may also fail to see real quality in quantitative group conversions. Of course, the danger of spiritual superficiality in a great movement must be recognized and cannot be minimized; but neither can the capacity of the Holy Spirit be minimized who performs the work of regeneration *in each* person, whether or not that person acts individually or collectively in the group.

Professor Tippett's concept of "multi-individual decision" or our concept of "multi-personal conversion" very appropriately describes what happens when a whole people or a homogeneous unit of a people becomes converted. Mission history and missiological case studies record many examples of such Christward movements. I am thinking of the Chols of Eastern India (Jellinghaus, 1874:24 f.), of the Papua and the Bullung peoples of New Guinea (Keysser, 1929; 1949:32-48), of the Gara people in a great revival (Pickett, 1973:21-35) and the "Mehra People Movement" of India (McGavran, 1973:71-83), and of the Maori Web conversion to Christ in Southern Polynesia (Tippett, 1971:40 f., 198 f.).

One of the outstanding examples of multi-personal conversion in recent years is that of the headhunting Sawi people of Dutch New Guinea, recorded by missionary Don Richardson in the fascinating book, *Peace Child* (1974). Richardson reports with a rare measure of cultural perception of the community spirit among the Sawi before and after their conversion. Promotion of Western individualism in that society would have been a direct violation of one of the people's most cohesive factors, namely that of communal decision-making. Richardson's record of the Sawi's Christian commitment offers rather convincing evidence that there, indeed, can be quality in quantity, for "all quantities are measurements of certain qualities" (Winter, 1972:177).

Quantity Through Quality

"In group conversion," says Warnshuis (1973:17-18), "the individual is still as important as ever. Groups are influenced through individuals." The same thought was expressed by Warneck's colleague and friend, professor Martin Kähler (1835-1912) of Halle, in his scholarly Christological essay on "The Son of Man and His Sentness to Mankind." In this essay Kähler stated that "the pathway to universalism is by individual persons and the pathway to mankind by each man" (1893:164). As the Apostle Paul lived for the conversion and spiritual welfare of the individual, said Kähler (1893:174), so he also labored with confidence for the conversion of the world. Warnshuis' contention that the group is influenced through the individual confirms that of the German missiologists, Warneck and Kähler. From the missiological perspective "the mistake occurs when the objective is only the individual who is separated from the group. Instead of separating him from the group, the individual should lead the way into the group" (Warnshuis, 1973:18).

The dimension of quality in New Testament conversions seems to have found its most appropriate expression in the phenomenon of *koinonia* (fellowship). Here the disciples demonstrated the test of quality in corporate quantitative action and response to God's will in the world for the building of His kingdom.

Summary

In the preaching of the gospel message with the purpose of bringing people to a conversion experience by accepting Christ as Savior from sin and as Lord of life, the objective is not a matter of *either-or* in terms of quality or quantity of converts, but *both*. Neither, however, can be achieved by accenting "individual conversion" in the sense of the philosophic understanding of individualism that has dominated Western Protestantism for too long. When one is converted he is converted as the self, as a person; but that always in *relational contexts* akin to his sociocultural environment. This relationship can best be expressed in terms of the triadical I-It, I-Thou, and I-You interactions as defined above. The principles of this interaction apply to both single conversions as well as group conversions.

An analysis of case studies in group conversion is beyond the scope of the present survey. Yet several observations gleaned from such studies will help to substantiate the thesis that the qualitative results of quantitative multipersonal conversions can be as natural and as genuine—often more lasting because of their communal nature—as single individual conversions when the latter tend to happen in isolation.

1. The missionary, as the advocate of change, must make deliberate efforts to direct the gospel message to the whole people, not only to individuals, as Keysser (1949:32 f.) and Vicedom (1962:124) have convincingly shown.

2. The nature of motivation for deciding to accept the gospel has little or no effect on the quality of converts who make a collective move toward Christianity. This is amply corroborated by Pickett's scientific studies (1933:152) of multi-personal conversions in South India.

3. The level of actual conversion from paganism to Christianity in the multipersonal group action of a communal society demands "encounter at some material locus of power at some specific point of time." Tippett refers to this as "a psychological moment or experience when the persons involved actually turn from the old god(s) to the new. There ought to be some ocular demonstration of this encounter, some specific act of faith" (1971:169).

4. Once the locus of power encounter has been fixed, a symbolic action by the chief in behalf of the group or by the whole group must take place—such as the burning of a fetish, the destruction of a grove, or the breaking of war spears—to indicate the change of loyalties from the old to the new way (cf. Keysser, 1949:39).

5. Whenever a group is strong, the fixing of the locus of power "tends to become a reference point for other groups

and individuals in a locality or within the social orbit" (Tippett, 1971:169). When this happens, the Holy Spirit continues his work of renewal and regeneration and the church begins to grow both in *quantity* and in *quality.*

The field in which the church lives and operates as a missionary church is the Fourth World, consisting of all unbelievers everywhere, whether pagan in a pre-Christian sense or neo-pagan in a post-Christian sense.

The missionary method which the church employs may be revitalization or renewal or both, depending on the existing ethnoreligious context, to which we must turn next.

Chapter 7

Revitalization and Renewal: An Ethnoreligious Concern

Nothing qualifies a man to speak to other men so much as the fact that he is a man.

—*R. Kenneth Strachan, 1964.*

The two concepts used to express the stated concern of this chapter are current in missiological writings. The one, "revitalization," is borrowed from anthropology, the other, "renewal," from ecclesiology. I have chosen these terms not as synonyms but as tools to delineate different types of conversion experiences, one touching the unchristianized pagan, the other the paganized or nominal Christian lifeway.

I will use the revitalization concept as defined by Professor Anthony Wallace (1956) of the University of Pennsylvania to delineate the Christianization process or conversion of pre-Christian pagans, and the renewal concept to describe the conversion experience of paganized Christians, or post-Christian neo-pagans.

Case Story: The Motilón Walked Jesus' Trail
"How can I walk on Jesus' trail?" Bobarishora (Bobby),

the leader-prophet of the tribe, asked Bruce (Bruchko) as they were sitting around the fire one evening. "No Motilón has ever done it. It's a new thing. There is no other Motilón to tell us how to do it" (Olson, 1973:159).°

The single missionary, Bruce Olson (1973:83-178) had spent ceaseless efforts, trying and failing to communicate the gospel in a way that would make sense among the savage Motilón tribe of the Colombian jungles. At the Festival of Arrows, the most significant Motilón festivity, the people exchanged arrows and had singing contests. Bruchko had joined them in their hammocks, but wanted to have one leg out with the foot on the ground for fear the strings might break. But he had quickly been informed that he must have both feet in the hammock and be fully suspended.

As they discussed this experience while walking on the trail, Bruchko found the answer for his Motilón friend. "You have to be suspended," he told him. "That is how it is when you follow Jesus, Bobby. No man can tell you how to walk His trail. Only Jesus can. But to find out you have to tie your hammock strings into Him, and be suspended in God."

The following day, Bobby joyfully told Bruchko that he had tied his hammock strings into Jesus. Then he added, "Now I speak a new language." What he meant was that he had a new way of speaking; that his speech henceforth would be Christ-oriented. For "to a Motilón, language is life." Bruchko now knew that Bobby had begun to walk with Jesus (Olson, 1973:160).

° The impact of the story can be gotten only by reading the book in its entirety. The case story, however, is based on chapters 10-19. Olson's book *For This Cross I'll Kill You*, together with Don Richardson's *Peace Child* is a reading must for all who want to know how God converts people in their cultural context.

Though fear and superstition had not yet left him completely, Bobby was singing a song that was different from all the rest. It was a song that helped him through the frightening night when the "tiger spoke" and the "spirits killed." He sang:

> Jesus is in my mouth;
> I have a new speech.
> Jesus is in my mouth;
> No one can take Him from me.
> I speak Jesus' words,
> I walk in Jesus' steps.
> I am a Jesus' boy;
> He has filled my stomach, and I am no longer hungry.
>
> (Olson, 1973:167)

There was to be another Festival of Arrows, a time when all Motilónes would gather to exchange arrows, form pacts, and have singing contests. Since their songs related legends, stories, and news items, they often lasted twelve hours, without interruption for food, drink, or rest.

An older chief, named Adjibacbayra, challenged Bobby to a song. He accepted. As they were swinging in a single hammock twenty feet off the ground, Bobby sang first; Adjibacbayra imitated line for line.

> Bobby's song was about the way the Motilónes had been deceived and had lost God's trail. He told how they had once known God, but had been greedy and had followed a false prophet. Then he began to sing about Jesus. As he did so, the other men who were singing stopped. Everyone became quiet in order to listen.
>
> "Jesus Christ was incarnated into man," Bobby sang. "He has walked our trails. He is God yet we can know Him" (Olson, 1973:168).

Obviously, Bobby had become an innovator. His work could result in social and religious revitalization within the Motilón way of life. And it did.

> Adjibacbayra looked at Bobby. "You've communicated a true news item," he said. "I too want to suspend myself in Jesus. I want to pull His blood over my deception."
>
> That night a spiritual revolution swept over the people. No one rejected the news about Jesus. . . . God had spoken. He had spoken in the Motilón language, and through the Motilón culture. He had not even had to use me (Olson, 1973:169).

The Revitalization Concept

One of the frequently quoted concepts in socioanthropological writings of the last two decades is Anthony Wallace's revitalization concept which appeared in the *American Anthropologist* (April 1956:264-281). Wallace declares that the term "revitalization" covers a variety of processes affecting both sociological and religious change:

> "Nativistic movement," "reform movement," "cargo cult," "religious revival," "messianic movement," "utopian community," "sect formation," "mass movement," "social movement," are some of the commonly used labels (1956:264).

The interesting hypothesis Wallace proposes is "that all organized religions are relics of old revitalization movements, surviving in routinized form in stabilized cultures, and the religious phenomena per se originated . . . in the revitalization process—i.e., in visions of a new way of life by individuals under extreme stress" (1956:268).

In order to understand Wallace's concept in the context of this study, I shall define and outline briefly his thesis and then construct a revitalization model in the form of a diagram. Wallace believes that the revitalization process is a

universal phenomenon which he defines "as a deliberate, organized, conscious effort by members of a society to
construct a more satisfying culture" (1956:256).

The Revitalization Process

In his analysis of Wallace's theory, anthropologist Robert
Ramseyer points out that revitalization as a culture-change
phenomenon presupposes certain attitudinal factors on the
part of the persons involved in the process: (1) They must
perceive of their culture as a system. (2) They must evidence
a sense of dissatisfaction with the existing system. (3) They
must make an effort to create a new cultural system, involving an abrupt change in relationships and to a new con-
figuration of traits (Ramseyer, 1970:151; Wallace,
1956:265). The case story of the Motilón is an example
where these principles apply. The process in itself consists of
a series of somewhat overlapping stages or periods.

1. The first stage Wallace calls "*the steady state*," which
means that the majority of people in the given social unit
still have the means to operate culturally efficient enough to
deal with stress situations—at least within tolerable limits—
within the culture system. In other words; they possess the
cultural techniques to satisfy and meet major needs that exist
in the group.

2. The second stage consists of a period of *increased personal stress* which emerges as a result of the decreased ability
to deal effectively with existing needs. Stress intensity rises at
the same rate as the ability to deal with it decreases. Such
factors as a military defeat, floral and faunal changes,
political subjection to foreign powers, pressures toward ac-
culturation resulting in internal culture conflict, and epi-
demic or economic distress may bring persons or groups of
persons to the point where they will consider an alternative

to their *modus operandi* within their culture. They may even
consider substituting an entirely new culture for the old as
Margaret Mead (1956) has shown. Yet the very consideration will increase the stress even more and pose a "threat of
mazeway disintegration" (Wallace, 1956:266), which is a
disintegration of a person's image of his own society, culture,
and self (Wallace, 1956:269).

3. This is followed by the third stage or period, namely
that of *cultural distortion*. As the ability diminishes to satisfy
needs adequately, the stress experience increases not only in
severity, but also in prolongation. When the failure of the attempt to adequately reduce stress becomes more and more
apparent, "and as the internal incongruities of the mazeway
are perceived, symptoms of anxiety over the loss of a meaningful way of life also become evident: disillusionment with
the mazeway, and apathy toward problems of adaptation,
set in" (Wallace, 1956:270).

4. This then sets the stage for the fourth period, namely
that of *revitalization* itself. Here Wallace lists six specific
functions which the religious revitalization process must
perform (see Figure 6):

(a) *Mazeway reformulation*. This presupposes a leader or
prophet within the group, such as Bobby among the Motilón
tribe. His particular function consists of a restructuring of
the elements and subsystems that become known to him.
The leader-prophet (also called "formulator") is involved in
the reformulation action. Prior to this, however, he experiences an abrupt and dramatic occasion which usually occurs "as a moment of insight, a brief period of realization of
relationships and opportunities," unknown heretofore
(Wallace, 1956:270). Now the situation is ripe for multi-personal conversion.

On the basis of this experience (which may be Christian

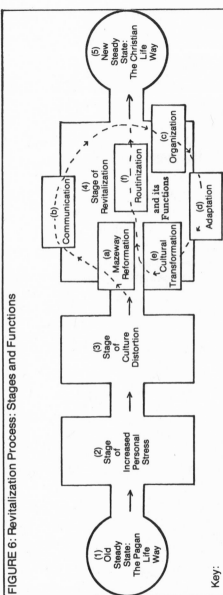

FIGURE 6: Revitalization Process: Stages and Functions

Key:

(1) The numbers (1) to (5) indicate the periods or stages of the revitalization process described by Wallace.

(2) The letters (a) to (f) in Stage (4) identify the functions of the revitalization process.

(3) The open circles of Stages (1) and (5) indicate the uncertainty of time with reference to the beginning and the termination of the two stages or periods respectively.

(4) The arrows between each stage not only show continuation of movement but also integration and overlapping of each stage in the process.

conversion), the prophet-leader formulates a code "which outlines both the construction of a utopian image of sociocultural organization and a transfer culture to progress from the present to the utopian condition" (Ramseyer, 1970:160; cf. Wallace, 1970:148). The prophet may act either alone or in collaboration with a number of other leaders to bring about the desired change of the mazeway and seek to harmonize the utopian image, received in a vision or dream, with the real image of the existing structure or *Gestalt* of self, society, and culture (Wallace, 1956:267).

(b) *Communication* is the second function in the revitalization process. The prophet-leader who operates as a man among men now becomes the prophet-innovator who communicates his experience to others who become his disciples and in turn tell still others. The content of their story is determined by their leader's experience. A chain reaction is set in motion and revitalization is in progress. Wherever the gospel has had sufficient impact, revitalization of society is actually Christianization of a people through multi-personal conversion.

(c) As soon as a sufficient number of people has responded to the prophet, "an embryonic campaign *organization* develops with three orders of personnel: the prophet; the disciples; and the followers" (Wallace, 1956:273). The crucial issue at this point is the use of charisma on the part of the leader. If he exercises his gift of leadership wisely and distributes leadership power in the new organization, the movement can go on; the prophet's or formulator's converted disciples then become the leaders. Wallace observes significantly at this point:

> As the group of converts expands, it differentiates into two parts: a set of disciples and a set of mass followers. The disciples

increasingly become the executive organization, responsible for administering the evangelistic program, protecting the formulator, combatting heresy, and so on. In this role the disciples increasingly become full-time specialists in work of the movement (1970:193).

(d) Any innovative, transforming movement will encounter resistance and thus use a variety of strategies to minimize objections. This is done by *adaptation* in the areas of "doctrinal modification; political and diplomatic maneuver; and force" (Wallace, 1956:274).

(e) Once *cultural transformation* takes place, chances are that the controlling portion of the movement succeeds in bringing about an organized program of group action. In a communal society, such as is described by Christian Keysser (1877-1961), for many years missionary in New Guinea (1949:32 f.), cultural transformation is deeply rooted in the world-view—the very core of the culture system—of the people involved. At this point the shift of loyalty becomes crucial. Where the leader-prophet has accepted Jesus Christ as Savior and Lord, there the disciples and followers will do likewise.

(f) If the preceding functions of the process are progressing satisfactorily, the final function will be that of *routinization*, which means that the group action "becomes established as normal in various economic, social, and political institutions and customs" (Wallace, 1956:275). Again, in a setting in which the gospel has become effective, the spiritual consequences will be far-reaching.

5. Thus the fourth stage with its cycle of functions has been completed and the revitalization movement enters its final period: *The New Steady State*. The culture of this state will likely be different in pattern and structure, traits and organizational operation from the earlier steady state.

While the transitional stages can best be characterized by instability and distortion, the new state is characterized by routinization and stability. Enormous changes have taken place in the process, changes affecting all areas of life and culture—even the very core of culture, the belief system. In other words, the process of revitalization has brought about a multi-personal conversion experience that has transformed the given society from its pagan context to a Christian way of life in which Jesus Christ is Lord, the church is the new community, and its members are the new disciples. Though the processes through the various stages have been described in terms of the sociocultural dynamics at work, the actual change was brought about by the Lord Jesus Christ and by the power of the Holy Spirit, as in the case of the Motilón.

Whenever Christian conversion occurs—be it in the sense of revitalization or in the sense of renewal—God's power to restore the *Imago Dei* to its proper position must be taken into account. After all, "conversion is an act of God. It is God building His Kingdom in the lives of people," as Paul Hiebert (1974:3) has said.

In *For This Cross I'll Kill You* (1973), Bruce Olson, messenger of Christ to the headhunting Motilónes of the South American highlands, writes about the great spiritual change that took place in the life of these people when they finally understood God's coming to them in Jesus. After describing the Motilón social system and natural way of life, Olson deals with their conversion, concluding that topic with these words:

> But with Jesus, there can be real change. Not just spiritual change. Not just change by and by. Real change, now, with visible power. He is the source of all change. He is the God of everyday miracles (1973:178).

Renewal and Conversion in Nominal Christianity

The term "renewal" is used in several ways to designate the process of making spiritually new what has become spiritually lax, lethargic, and lacking in Christian vitality. Thus Professor F. F. Bruce of Manchester University subtitled the concluding volume of his church history (1965) *Evangelical Renewal and Advance in the Nineteenth Century.* Bruce uses the term "renewal" to mean the same as Dr. J. Edwin Orr's concept of "revival" and "awakening" (1973:55), which Orr also defines as "the revitalizing of the lives of nominal Christians" (1973:VII). Renewal in the church brings new life to its members and causes paganized Christians of nominal, institutionalized Christianity to seek meaning and new life in Christ.

There are levels of nominal Christianity, but they are difficult to measure. To do that, empirical data would have to be gathered and analyzed which is beyond the scope of this study. In this study renewal is used to describe only two specific situations of nominal Christians.

Renewal as Restoration and Reformation

Renewal is the reconversion of a nominal Christian who has "erred from the truth" (James 5:19) and thus reverted from faith to non-faith. In other words, renewal is used for the experience of restoration of a "backslider" to God or for "converting the sinner from the error of his way," in the words of James 5:20, to the way of truth and discipleship. In this sense, renewal means a return to the will of God and to the acquisition of the true knowledge of God, the true Christian faith, the genuine relationship with God and humanity, the abundant life in Christ, and a life under the guidance and control of the Holy Spirit; it means the restoration of the *Imago Dei* in the sinner, "the reestablishment of the

Kingdom of Heaven," as the Dutch theologian H. W. Meihuizen has said (1970:142); it means the restitution of a
person to a life of discipleship under the lordship of Christ.

Renewal also means religious reformation of a total,
inadequate ecclesiological belief system—or a part of that
system—with the objective of changing the system to a way
of life conducive to faith, action, and fullness of life according
to the gospels; it means revival as the moving of the Spirit of
God upon the hearts of people *en masse* to live a life in ac-
cordance with God's will; it means restitution as "the return
of the church to her original state as the apostolic congregation" (Meihuizen, 1970:142).

Renewal and Conversion in Ethno-Religious Perspectives

Professor Homer Barnett of the University of Oregon has
helped us to understand the respective roles of the advocate
and the innovator in bringing about decision-making and
change (1965:62-64). Dr. Tippett, a former student of
Barnett, has applied these principles to renewal, conversion,
and church growth. He speaks of "change by *directed advocacy*" and points to the divine as well as the human side of
it. Both sides must be considered in every renewal movement within the nominal church, which we have called "paganized Christianity," or *Verheidnischung der Kirche*," as
Hans Schärer (1937:48 f.) has put it.

Tippet offers some noteworthy observations:

> We realize that God is at work in the situation; that in the
> last analysis it is God who converts people; that we men can
> never "save" anyone or make them into new creatures. Science
> and psychology have not yet explained the precise nature of
> that change in man when he is converted. It is an observable,
> but unexplained change.
>
> But there is another side of the conversion process which I

am calling the human side. As long as we believe we are called to mission we are advocates, and in this respect anthropology has something to say to us. Anthropology is not concerned with conversion of men to Christ, except as an academic study, but it does study how men make decisions and how they act upon those decisions once they have been made. It also shows us the difference between effective and ineffective relationships of the advocate to the acceptor. It shows us what kind of advocacy is likely to meet with obstruction and rejection or acceptance. In other words, anthropology can tell us many things about how the gospel might be more effectively presented (Tippett, 1973:122).

Tippett furthermore suggests several specific insights from anthropological theory that are operative in any human decision-making process, including that of renewal and conversion in organized and institutionalized Christendom (1973:122-29).

Whereas the agent or advocate of change is usually an outsider to the group making the decision, the innovator works within to bring about change being advocated. In the ecclesiological context, the advocate may be an evangelist, a prophet, a teacher, a preacher, a witness who proclaims what he feels called or compelled to proclaim. In the case of Paul it was both. He was called by God to preach Christ and he felt compelled to be His ambassador (1 Corinthians 1:1; 2:1 f.; 2 Corinthians 5:14 f.).

The most significant thing to remember is, as Tippett reminds us, that effective and positive change (conversion) occurs whenever two compatible factors converge: (a) The situation must be ripe for change and (b) the change agent or advocate has a specific message which is relevant to the given situation (Tippett, 1973:122).

We may recall instances from ecclesiastical history that illustrate the point. When Girolamo Savonarola (1452-1498) came to Florence in 1481 and preached the gospel, the situation was ripe for change and people were converted. When Ulrich Zwingli (1484-1531) began to preach the Word of God in Zurich in the early 1520s, great ecclesiastical changes took place, disciples gathered around him and carried on the work (Blanke, 1961:7-20). When Menno Simons (1492-1561) of Witmarsum (Holland) went to Germany subsequent to his own conversion in 1536, thousands of Germans responded to his preaching and were converted. When the great Pietist preacher Edward Wüst (1818-1859) went to Russia in 1845 to preach among German settlers there, a great renewal movement emerged among both Lutherans and Mennonites, resulting in the formation of the Mennonite Brethren Church in 1860 (P.M. Friesen, 1911:168 f.) and in numerous home Bible study groups, known as *Stundisten*.

The history of the Evangelical Awakenings and the great renewal movements in Protestant nominalism also give ample evidence that spiritual change and transformation take place whenever the change agent and the ripe situation converge at a given point of time and space.

Acceptance/Rejection Potential

Every movement in every decision-making process has the capacity and potential to accept or to reject the options available to it.

1. There is the possibility of *total rejection*. The factors are many. Psychologically, the time may be premature to press for a verdict on the part of the advocate. Or sociologically, the time may be inopportune due to lack of proper advocacy or appropriate communication beforehand. All major resistance factors must first be overcome to minimize the rejection potential.

2. In other situations there may be *total acceptance*. Generally, this is a rare happening and not always healthy when it does occur. "Normal acceptors want to modify something," as Tippett points out. He continues, "I begin to question the salesmanship, or the honesty of the advertising, or to wonder if there were some subtle pressures behind this 'package deal,' or some exploitation of circumstances" (Tippett, 1973:125). This puts great responsibility on the advocate. To promise nominal Christians within any type of institutionalized Christendom, be it Catholic or Protestant, that to submit to the lordship of Christ in a renewal or conversion act means an end to all problems of health, poverty, animosity, etc., is first-degree deception. People who become converted in order to get material and physical gain in return may be very disappointed. Discipleship is a costly affair; it promises no easy road, no material gain.

3. There is a third form of acceptance, namely "*acceptance with modification*" (Tippett, 1973:126). This form seems to be most normal and effective. This is particularly the case when it comes to modification of the form, the way the message is conveyed, not the content of the message. The form is simply the medium used to convey the message. The content of the message must be carefully guarded, lest syncretism or a paganized form of Christianity (Luzbetak, 1970:239-48) evolves. The content must be biblical, but without Western, non-biblical trimmings.

If we have confidence in the Holy Spirit, He will apply the content to all new situations, so that a truly new lifestyle can emerge. The form, on the other hand, may often remain unchanged or be only slightly modified. In fact, the Spirit of God may choose to employ different forms or media natural or indigenous to the existing structure. But He will fill these forms with new meaning and life.

Levels of Change and Renewal

The process of change or renewal itself has several levels, which I shall refer to as "points" and "periods." The message of the evangelist or missionary or preacher, who fills the role of the change agent or advocate from the outgroup, takes the message first to the leaders or innovators of the ingroup. In most communal societies the innovators will carry on the work toward affecting the desired change. In Western societies the advocate may continue, without the aid of innovators, bringing the message directly to the masses who are the subjects of change. In either case change is more likely to take place than not.

Specific periods are discernible in the process of decision-making and change. To describe this process the designation of "period" and "point" may be used, following step by step the patterns interwoven in the existing cultural or ecclesiastical structures. "I want to stress that this is a *process*," Tippett contends, "and that the evangelist, whether a missionary or a national, needs to bring the group along step by step." Every process of decision-making—whether it is individual as in most Western societies or multi-personal as in most non-Western cultures—must lead from mere awareness and cognitive levels to a climax "in a clear-cut encounter, a definite verdict for Christ." This must be followed by directed incorporation (Tippett, 1973:134) and inward maturation (Tippett, 1974:4). The result will be internalization of the changing and dynamic message received until that message becomes a verbal and demonstrative testimony of the new Christian to the Fourth World around him.

Adapting Tippett's modified "processual model" (Figure 7) for conversion in totally non-Christian settings, I wish to note the following periods and points in the renewal process from nominal Christianity to Christian discipleship.

1. Period One, Points R-O. This is the period of *awareness that there is an option*. When the gospel is preached and the Holy Spirit convicts people of their sinfulness, they come to the point of *realization* of an *option*, or "R-O," namely that there is another way, the Christian way of discipleship.

2. Period Two, Points E-C. Without the realization that life can be more meaningful and abundant than hitherto experienced and known, there could be no second period. But once awareness reaches the point where the persons realize their plight caused by sin, stress, or felt needs, the decision-making period is initiated by the point of *encounter* and climaxes in the point of *commitment*, or "E-C."

3. Period Three, Points F-B. As soon as the decision has been made to change from the old to the new way and the new way has been accepted at points E-C, there follows a period in which that change is evidenced. This will include believer's baptism and incorporation into a new community, the believers' church. Here the new believer touches for the first time in his life a new context of community. He experiences *fellowship* and *belongingness*; he feels at-homeness, points "F-B."

4. Period Four, Points I-M. As Tippett points out in his "Research in Progress Pamphlet #13" (1974:4-5), the fourth period is open-ended. The Christian grows in grace, experiences assurance of his new birth, and enters what the pietists used to call Heiligung, a life of sanctification. Here the power of the Holy Spirit becomes evident in spiritual "dynamitization." Thus the points at which the new disciple of Jesus Christ touches *internalization* of truth and *maturation* in truth and grace becomes lines of growth until he reaches "unto the measure of the stature of the fullness of Christ" Himself (Ephesians 4:13; see Figure 7 on page 40).

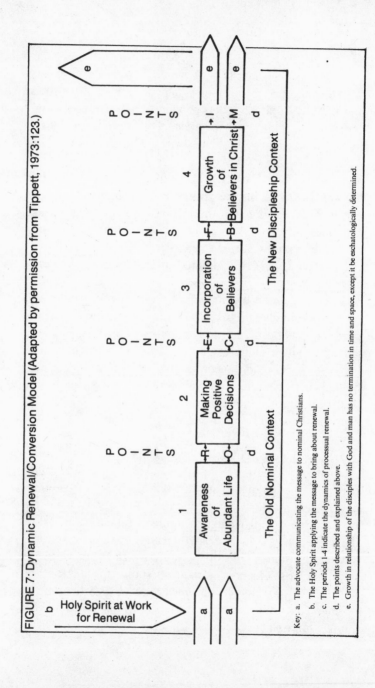

FIGURE 7: Dynamic Renewal/Conversion Model (Adapted by permission from Tippett, 1973:123.)

Holy Spirit at Work for Renewal

1	2	3	4
Awareness of Abundant Life	Making Positive Decisions	Incorporation of Believers	Growth of Believers in Christ

The Old Nominal Context

The New Discipleship Context

Key: a. The advocate communicating the message to nominal Christians.
      b. The Holy Spirit applying the message to bring about renewal.
      c. The periods 1-4 indicate the dynamics of processual renewal.
      d. The points described and explained above.
      e. Growth in relationship of the disciples with God and man has no termination in time and space, except it be eschatologically determined.

Summary

To summarize briefly our understanding of revitalization
and renewal, we may say that revitalization describes the
conversion process as a religious change of an ethnological
system from its pagan context to the Christian way of life. It
proceeds along lines of inherent principles operative in
multi-personal decisions within an entire belief system or
subsystem; this belief system becomes the subject of change
from the *old steady state*, with emerging culture distortions
decreasingly capable of solving its mounting problems, to a
new steady state capable of solving adequately the problems
and of meeting existing needs of the society which has opted
for the new way of life.

The concept of renewal has been applied to describe the
spiritual restoration of reverted and paganized Christians or
post-Christian neopagans; it refers to the transformation of
such nominal Christians both within the camp of second-,
third-, fourth-, or tenth-generation Christianity as well as
within the context of neopaganism. Although I recognize
that there are different levels of nominal Christianity and
degrees of neopaganism, it is beyond the scope of this study
to deal with those levels and with the different conversion
experiences parallel to each of these levels.

The diagrams following the description of revitalization
(Figure 6, page 129), and of renewal (Figure 7), are an attempt to illustrate the dynamics operative in Christian
conversion within the stated contexts.

It is hardly necessary to underscore that Christian conversion as understood in this study is not a static, but a dynamic
experience. The highlight of that experience is when a
person realizes that he has become a child of God. Beyond
that, however, change is an ongoing process; it is never complete until a Christian reaches perfection which, according

to the ethnotheological understanding of this study, is reached only when the powers of evil and sin have been fully overcome and the disciples of Christ have reached their fullness in Him. That eschatological event will come when Christ the Lord will present the church to Himself as "a glorious church, not having spot or wrinkle" (Ephesians 5:27). Therefore, the conversion models are open-ended, leaving room for the ongoing dynamic of growth in grace through the Word by the power of the Holy Spirit. Relational growth of discipleship under the lordship of Christ is ongoing and unending until the Lord Himself terminates it by bringing His believing disciples to the *pleroma*, the fullness in Himself (Colossians 2:19).

The problem that arises in preaching for a verdict which brings about conversion of people to God is whether those within a nominal Christian or semi-Christian context need to be converted. Is it not sufficient—as some would say—to make a verbal confession to Christ? This is a real concern from generation to generation within Christendom, a concern that demands our immediate attention.

Chapter 8

Conversion or Confession: A Generational Concern

Regenerated people have a spiritual king over them who rules them by the unbroken sceptre of His mouth, namely, with His Holy Spirit and Word.

—*Menno Simons*, ca 1537 (1956).

In a provocative chapter of his *Reden und Aufsätze* the renowned missiologist Walter Freytag (1899-1959) deals with "The Problem of the Second Generation in the Young Church" (1961, I:245-58). He defines "second generation" not in terms of biological chronology, but in terms of Christian heritage, conversion, and the Christian way of life. In that sense second-generation Christians—or third-, fourth-, or fifth-generation Christians—consist of those people who have accepted a set of Christian beliefs inherent in institutionalized Christendom. Such acceptance is not made by virtue of a personal conversion to Christ, but by virtue of a Christian heritage. Thus the status of second-generation Christians essentially depends on the decision made by the first generation—their parents or any generation before them.

Any form of institutionalized Christianity—whether it be Mennonite or Reformed, Lutheran or Baptist—must be particularly perceptive to the Spirit of God who seeks to convict of sin and to perform the miracle of Christian conversion and regeneration. Mere assent to a creed, even if supplemented by good works, is no substitute for conversion.

Case Story: A Widow in Paraguay
Experiences Conversion

"Mother dear, now I'm different."

With these words my son Alverto greeted me when he returned from a Mennonite Brethren youth conference held in São Paulo in February of this year [1976].

"Why is that?" I asked. "Because I received Christ into my heart," he explained.

I wept for joy because his words touched the most intimate fiber of a mother's feelings and with a great deal of emotion I told him,

"I have Him in my heart ever since I was a little girl."

It seemed to me like a miracle that the two of us should now be united by the love of God.

With these words the widow Señora Irma Zelada de Arza of Pirayu, Paraguay,° began to relate her conversion story to a large audience at the Christian conference grounds in San Bernardino, Paraguay. She continued, saying,

Today I am at a conference myself. The first day I felt somewhat strange among so many strange people. However, as we sang and prayed together I sensed that we were all one in the love of Christ. . . .

As the days went by, and I listened to the Scriptures, I began

---

°I have translated the case story, including the poem, from the Spanish. Señora de Arza related her conversion in my hearing; she also gave it in writing. Original in my files.

to realize that I lacked something. Despite the fact that I loved God, believed that Christ had died for me on the cross, performed good works in order to please Him, I knew there was something missing.

Then we read in the Bible about a man, Nicodemus. He was a person who also believed, loved, and served God, just as I did. Yet he could not have salvation unless he were born anew. This opened my eyes to a great truth. Right then I was born again as I put aside my old, sinful ego and received Jesus as my Savior. Now I believe His Word. I am certain I have found the way that leads to heaven (cf. Arza, 1976:5).

A few months later we visited Mrs. Arza in her home. She had invited the whole neighborhood, including the commissioner and the judge of Pirayu. She told of her spiritual pilgrimage "From Poverty to Wealth" and concluded with these lines:

From Poverty to Wealth

Destitute was I and starving for love;
My innermost was thirsty for a faithful friend.
Now I have found Him whom I was searching
To forgive and save me just as I was.

Never had I thought that I could be so wealthy;
I never could think it, no never—
That ever I should find so great a treasure,
A treasure no money could buy.

God loves me, I know, He loves me so much,
So much that He gives me all things.
I know I have everything, nothing I lack.
I have everything—I have His love.

No longer fear I evil in this ungrateful world,
No longer I starve; no longer I thirst.

He satisfies—fills me with goodness;
He fills me with gladness and joy.

No one can ever rob my beautiful jewel,
The treasure I hold in my heart.
The key to that treasure in heaven is guarded,
My Bible is passport to that.

Religious Institutionalization

In his book, *Cultural Anthropology*, Professor Paul Hiebert (1976:253-57) very effectively delineates what he terms the "process of institutionalization" (Figure 8). Hiebert shows how this process is capable of transforming any new movement within the larger social order into an integral part of the traditional structure. Normally, at least three stages can be distinguished in the process of institutionalization: (a) Formalization, which may be described as the transformation of the informal beliefs and practices of the founders into standard practices and dogmas of their followers; (b) self-maintenance occurs when the leaders see personal advantage in the existing patterns and become concerned with maintaining the same; (c) traditionalism results when the system becomes established in the social order and infused with the social values.

In religious movements formalization seems to be the stage with the profoundest impact in the process. Take, for example, the Anabaptist movement of the sixteenth-century reformation. Its leadership can be defined as charismatic in character, rather than in terms of specializations. Its organization was informal, rather than rigidly structured. Its theology was implicit rather than explicit in systematic format. Its activities were need-oriented, rather than show-oriented. Its membership was voluntary and dynamic, rather than coercive and stalemated. Its lifestyle was simple and

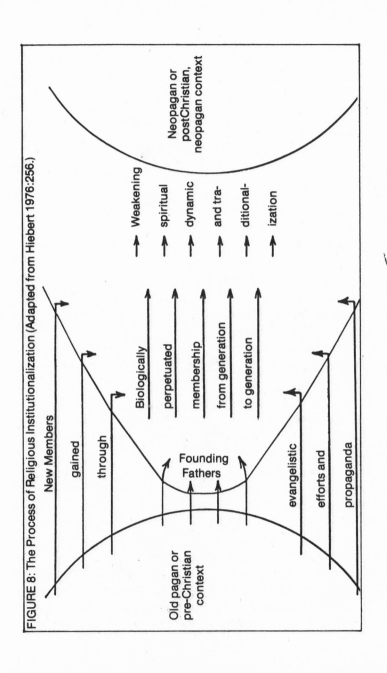

FIGURE 8: The Process of Religious Institutionalization (Adapted from Hiebert 1976:256.)

submissive, commensurate with true discipleship under Christ's lordship, rather than assuming and dominating. But much of that changed with the third- and fourth-generations when self-maintenance gained high priority and the ingredients of true discipleship of the first generation were transformed into a system of established traditionalism. Almost any American denomination would fall into a similar pattern. Hiebert's description of the process is significant and noteworthy:

> Formalization results when the informal customs and beliefs of the founders are transformed into the accepted practices and explicit dogmas of their followers. For instance, leadership in informal groups is often vested in charismatic spokesmen, who inspire others to action. As the need for organization grows, there is increasing specialization of labor and the formation of specific leadership roles. Ways must be developed to insure continuity of leadership and to invest in it the authority to enforce decisions. Thus, leadership becomes identified with formal offices.
>
> The shift of leadership from individuals to offices is particularly difficult when the founding fathers are strong charismatic leaders, whose decisions are accepted with little question. Their successors are often caught in the thankless task of creating formal leadership roles that are stable and efficient, even though they lack the charisma and popular appeal of the founders (Hiebert, 1976:254-55).

As we have seen earlier, the way to spiritual life and dynamic discipleship is Christian conversion or regeneration. Thus every generation must not only guard its spiritual development and the many changes that it is called upon to make; it must be open to the Holy Spirit, who seeks to transform every member of each generation into the image of Christ, not to traditionalism.

Characteristic Tendencies of Third World Nominalism

Historically, second-generation Christians are potential first-generation Christians, depending on the length of time it takes for the cycle of evolution to move from pre-Christian paganism to Christianity and from Christianity to post-Christian neopaganism. Any great spiritual renewal movement within institutionalized nominal Christendom may produce first-generation Christians as genuinely as a revitalization movement which may result in Christian conversion within an authentically pagan context.

The anthropological principles outlined by Professor Hiebert can be seen in actual operation in an institutionalized church. From a case study in Indonesia, Walter Freytag (1961, I:248-51) states and describes four characteristic tendencies in the nominality of second-generation Christians in that country.

A Negative Ethic in Daily Living

The first characteristic is a negative ethic. The Christians have learned to say "no" to certain pagan practices. By their abstinence from participation in such direct *acts* as blood revenge, polygamy, witchcraft, and sacrifice to ancestral spirits, they believe to demonstrate their Christian commitment. Yet Freytag rightly points out that people can be fearfully superstitious without practicing witchcraft; they can pay close attention to omens without carrying amulets on their bodies; they can fear or respect evil spirits without worshiping them. In all of this, however, there are positive possibilities for spiritual renewal without having to overcome the many habits and vices rampant in pre-Christian paganism.

Habitual Form Christianity

A second characteristic of second-generation Christians is a kind of imitated, habitual form Christianity.

> Just as the pagans lived in traditional practice which they inherited from their ancestors and imitated without ever critically questioning their validity, so there are church customs that have become an integral part of the religious way of life without ever seriously evaluating their value and, consequently, without the benefit of spiritual fruit (Freytag, 1968:249).

But even in these customs, Freytag sees a positive note with reference to Hebrews 5:14 where we read that the participants' faculties are trained by practice [Gewohnheit = habit] to distinguish good from evil. That same principle was also noted in the case story of this chapter.

Law Without Spirit

The third characteristic of second-generation Christians is the tendency to be legalistic. The second generation is less concerned with what the professing followers ought to *be* as Christians than with what they should *do* because of what they are. These people are aware of the norms their community established during first-generation Christian days, the days of "first love" to Christ and to the members of that community. But some of these norms now seem obsolete to the second-generation Christians. They simply consider such irrelevant norms imposed on them from the past. In their concern, they adopt subtle ways of scheming as to what they *can afford doing* without the risk of being punished for violating a given rule which by now lacks brotherhood consensus within their own community.

Such casuistic tendencies have several inherent problems for the individual, the community, or Christian church of which the individual is a member.

1. There is the failure to differentiate between what we might call "culture sins" and "Bible sins." The former may be defined as infractions of those cultural norms and social mores on which the first generation church reached consensus long ago in different times and different cultural settings, but which for the second-generation Christians are by common consensus no longer defined as sins. "Bible sins," on the other hand, are of two kinds, but always knowable and known. The one kind is clearly defined by the Ten Commandments; the other is determined by the "ethical discernment of the local Christian community to which we belong" and by our relationship to that community, as professor John E. Toews of the Biblical Seminary, Fresno, has put it (1975:6).

2. A second problem arises when violators of certain traditional rules, cultural norms, social mores, and Bible sins have to be corrected by the local Christian community, resulting neither in conviction nor in change on the part of those disciplined. They accept disciplinary measures as the consequence of sinful action rather than reject sinful action as the result of attempted correction. The question then arises as to whether the violator was unaware of this unacceptable action because the ethical standards and sins were not clearly defined by his Christian community, or whether the pleasure derived from infraction of a stated known rule was worth the consequential, inevitable punishment.

But even in such legalistic circumstances Freytag (1961, I:250) sees the potential to raise the deeper question as to what is right and what is wrong in the sight of God. But whenever that is the case, the need arises for a "second conversion," as missionary Johannes Warneck (1867-1944) has said (cf. Delius, 1940:265). Or it may be the need for "resocialization," as Jacob Loewen calls the process beyond the stage of initial conversion. The need for such experience is not only felt, but often desired and expressed.

> The commonly professed ideal for socialization as Christians is a conversion experience that so transforms the individual's inner nature that the convert henceforth under the guidance of the Spirit of God fulfills all the behavioral standards laid down in the Word of God. In actual experience, however, converts in every society, including our own, usually need a context which will help them actualize the Christian ideals they profess. Such expressions as "to grow in grace," "to gain victory over evil habits," and "to learn to demonstrate the fruits of the Spirit" indicate the need for Christian socialization even beyond conversion (Loewen, 1968:193).

Christian in Form but Pagan in Meaning

A fourth characteristic of second-generation Christians is the fact that they often carry their faith in pagan thought patterns.

Dr. Th. Ahrens of the Melanesian Institute for Pastoral and Socio-Economic Service has shown that the Lutheran Christians in Papua, New Guinea, after eighty years of missionary influence, have developed their own concept of Christianity. When the Bugatis, for example, were converted they made a clean break with their pagan past. This was upheld in the first generation. But in the third and fourth generation Ahrens observes a reawakening and resurfacing of indigenous traditions (1975:180 ff.). What this means, as Freytag shows, is that church members begin to revert to old thought patterns, explaining Christian forms in terms of pagan meanings. This results in a higher degree of syncretism than that evidenced by the first generation. Second-generation Christians are more concerned about *dying* as Christians in order to have a secure and blissful hereafter than they are about *living* as Christians here and now by paying the high cost of discipleship (cf. Freytag, 1961:251). More emphasis is placed on confessing a creed and on participating in the sacraments than on living in the will of God.

The Western Church's Third World Problems

The principles of the above theses from Third World contexts can also be carried over into and applied to any nominal church situation in the West in which biological growth has been the major means of perpetuating church membership. The key issue in Freytag's analysis of an Indonesian nominal Christian church is, therefore, not different from that of second-, third-, or fourth-generation churches elsewhere in the world. The problem may be that of a learned confession without an experienced conversion; it may be that of substituting good deeds for conversion, as the case story of this chapter shows; it may also be a combination of both.

This issue has been dealt with in similar studies made by missionary anthropologist Jacob Loewen, professor Delbert Wiens of Pacific College, missionary Herman Buehler of Truk Island, the Methodist pastor Robert Raines, and others.

Wiens essay *New Wineskins for Old Wine* (1965), Loewen's numerous articles in *Practical Anthropology* (1960-1973) and other journals, and Buehler's thesis on "Nominality Considered" (1973), as well as Raines' *New Life in the Church*, all provide significant insight into the problems encountered by what Freytag called "second-generation Christians."

The real question is, "Do they experience actual conversion and transformation of life or do they simply repeat the verbal confession of their Christian forebears?" Confession of a creed is no substitute for a commitment to Christ as Savior and Lord. In biblical jargon a "second conversion" (which is actually a first conversion, as I will show shortly) or the "process of resocialization" is called "being born again" or the "new birth" (John 3:1-8). That is why Donald A. McGavran and his colleagues of the church Growth School of Thought insist that biological growth alone is inadequate and that each second- or third-generation Christian in the Orient as well as in the Occident must face a personal confrontation in which he not only decides to believe or not to believe in the faith of his fathers, to confess or not to confess the creed of his forebears; he must also decide to live or not to live, to be or not to be for or against Jesus, the Lord. Thus, speaking of biological growth as a basic principle of church growth, professor Tippett perceptively explains what this means, namely,

> that each generation of people born to Christians needs to be brought to Christ itself by some act of definite commitment. The more a church depends on its young people graduating into membership, without some point of encounter, the more that church is likely to be troubled with nominality (1973:10).

From Pagan to Neopagan: A Generational Cycle

By now it has become clear that the generational concerns must take seriously conversion practices as well as creedal confessions.

The Way of Generations

First-generation Christians have been converted either from paganism or from neopaganism to Christianity. Their break with the old ways and practices was clear-cut. Their conversion—whether individually personal or multi-personal—was demonstrative of a dramatic change in their entire lifeway. Old habits and practices have passed away; all things have become new.

Even though the forms and structures indigenous to their culture are maintained to express their new life in Christ, the content of that life itself is as close to being wholly scriptural as possible, commensurate with the new lifeway in the old culture. By and large, syncretism has been kept to a minimum. The conversion experience was a highly visible, dramatic change of life. Normal growth in Christian lifeways is the result. The point of conversion itself, as Wiens puts it, "was in the once-in-a-lifetime wrenching that guaranteed their new status." They have, indeed, placed themselves on a new road. They have turned around. They have been converted (Wiens, 1965:6), as we have shown by Type B above.

But now the second-, third- or fourth-generation comes along and the conversion pattern of the forefathers hardly applies to their descendants. First-generation Christians became what they are now through a deep religious experience; they became what they are in "one big jump," as it were. But to force the children to repeat the conversion patterns appropriate for adult pagans or neo-pagans is to distort the genuine relationship with God that the child is experiencing in the Christian home. True, the child must be born again, but hardly in a cataclysmic fashion.

Course of Action

Robert Raines has some noteworthy observations primarily relevant to Western society, which we affirm at this point:

> Most of those persons who have grown up within the church have been zigzagging along in the general direction of Christ.

Early in life they were positioned toward Christ, and they have been meandering His way more or less ever since. If asked, "Are you Christian?" they would say, "Of course. All respectable people are." If asked, "Have you decided for Christ?" They would grow uneasy and look around for the door.

And then something happens—that marvelous, fresh time of awakening to decision, when you stop meandering, and make choices (1961:44-45).

That "time of awakening" to which Raines refers may be the result of several courses of action taken by the people involved. For one it may be an uneventful path leading to the point of commitment. For another it may be a hard road of repeated decisions to follow Christ without ever really knowing the implications of discipleship. For still another it may have been preceded by a time of open rebellion, deliberate waywardness, and conscious, voluntary alienation from the way in order to "taste the world" and what it has to offer before deciding to follow Christ. This latter experience may be undesirable, yet not unrealistic. This makes Wiens' contention all the more true when he confirms,

The children must be converted as their parents were converted; "they must be born from above." But a deeper understanding of the meaning of conversion is needed if the young are to escape the need for a shallow kind of half-deliberate rebellion so that "grace may abound to them also" (1965:7).

To make the conversion pattern of pagan adults binding for second-generation children raised in first-generation Christian homes is not only to misunderstand conversion, but also to deny that God meets every generation at every level of life and experience within their time span and sociocultural context.

The children raised by godly parents in Christian homes

do not need to become pagan in order to experience a genuine conversion (see Case Story of a Weaver, Chapter 4, above), just as the Gentiles in the apostolic era were not required to become Jews in order to become Christian (Acts 15). By the same token, however, they must be converted at their level of life experience, lest they simply repeat a confession or a creed and remain or become nominal, institutionalized Christians, which I have referred to as "post-Christian neopagans." This type of conversion of "Christians" in Christian homes—the voluntary commitment to Christ as Lord—is what Johannes Warneck has referred to as "a second conversion" (Delius, 1940:265).

The path from nominal Christianity to neopaganism and assimilation back into culture is short and the boundaries are often unmarked. In fact, it seems much more difficult to convert from pre-Christian paganism to true Christian discipleship than to revert from Christianity to post-Christian neopaganism, though the latter may be a longer road in terms of time. The path of de-Christianization runs parallel with re-paganization and hardly stops short of paganism itself.

Seriousness of the Problem

When second- or third-generation children in Christian homes are forced to demonstrate a conversion pattern comparable to that of the first-generation Christians who converted from paganism, they will often revert to sinful, godless living in order to demonstrate satisfactorily their conversion experience to their forebears. Their road to neopaganism may have been a very costly one. Alas, only after sinful practices are they all too often able to authenticate to their elders a dramatic conversion experience that becomes the only criterion for genuineness. But such a route is

undesirable. What they need is Christian nurture in order to
help them arrive at a gradual conversion experience, described above and illustrated in Figure 3, Type A (Page 76).

The problem for second-generation Christians is a serious
one. For one thing, first-generation Christians all too often
lack what Wiens calls a "theology of Christian nurture" to
help their children cope adequately with spiritual problems.
Furthermore, first-generation Christians "know what to do
with pagans but not what to do with [their] own children"
(Wiens, 1965:7). The problem is even compounded when
we take into account the inherent "tendency for reversion"
in second- and third-generation Christians. Michael Griffiths, director of Overseas Missionary Fellowship, calls the
church of the young generation the "church in retreat" also
characteristic of paganized Christianity of Europe and
America (Griffiths, 1972:28).

From a missiological perspective this means that the first-
generation church of Africa, Asia, and Latin America should
send its evangelists to the old churches in Europe and Anglo-
America. These non-Western missionaries should help the
second- and third-generation Christians in the West to once
again get hold of the gospel of repentance and become
converted to Christ, lest they continue blindly repeating a
creed without the new birth and a life of discipleship.

Thus it becomes clear that the danger in second- and
third-generation Christians is to repeat a creed as a confession of faith without both the appropriate Christian nurture and true conversion. This route leads to nominality and
institutionalized Christendom, which by its very nature, is a
type of neopaganism. By virtue of its creedal confession, it
appears as a form of godliness, yet by its action, it denies the
power of godly essence. When that happens, renewal-
conversion is a way back to God. The other route is that of

open rebellion and sin in which a sudden, cataclysmic conversion experience can take place.

Such are the ways on which second-, third- or fourth-generation "paganized Christians" can become first-generation believers and disciples of Jesus Christ, the Lord.

Conversion of First-Generation Christians

Wiens mentions "two ways to think about conversion" (1965:4), one experiential and subjective, the other doctrinal and objective. The subjective conversion experience of first-generation Christians was one of agony and struggle in the power encounter between the *Imago Dei* in humankind and the drives to sin in fallen humanity. This is the conflict between the two powers: God—humankind's Creator, and the devil—humankind's deceiver; between good and evil, holiness and sinfulness. Faust, the protagonist in Goethe's classical drama, describes this conflict when he speaks to his Christian counselor of the two natures or the two souls in man:

> With passion's drives you are by only one possessed;
> Would that you not admit another to a share.
> Two souls, alas, are dwelling in my breast,
> Each wrestling to gain throne and mastery there.
> The one is lured by passions crude for lust
> And hugs the world with all its sensuous rage;
> The other tears itself from murky dust
> To seek above a lofty heritage.

(Goethe's *Faust* I, 1957:146,
translation mine.)

Accounts of revivals and revitalization movements, both resulting in first-generation converts, give evidence of the struggles and conflicts that take place in personal as well as in multi-personal decisions. Testimonies like these are common:

> For two weeks (three weeks, four weeks) I struggled with God. I could not eat or sleep. I felt that hell was swallowing me up. Then one day I could not stand it any longer. I stopped the horses and threw myself beside the plow and gave myself to God. Then, oh, the peace that came over me when my sins rolled away (Wiens, 1965:4).

Wiens observes on individual conversion experiences among the early Mennonite Brethren in Russia, saying,

> Although there were individual differences here, they discovered that they could reduce the subjective side of the experience to a general pattern. First, they had felt lost, empty, dissatisfied. This led to search for God. But contemplation of God revealed not only emptiness but also sin, self-assertion, guilt. And then came a violent struggle to "give in" to God, followed by a shattering experience (the climax with a verdict in the power encounter) and then peace (Wiens, 1965:4).

But the subjective experience has an objective side to it also. The new convert who has been transformed by the power of the Spirit of God does not only seek to explain what has happened to him subjectively, experientially; he also seeks to explain objectively in terms of truths rooted in the Scriptures what the experience is all about. He seeks to describe it in doctrinal terms which become his creed, his confession, his dogma.

The objective factors which first-generation converts deem essential, as Wiens (1965:5) leads us to observe, are: God exists. He is always creatively and redemptively active. He has revealed Himself in Scripture, in nature, and, above all, in His Son. He has created humanity, moral beings, in

His image. Humanity has fallen into sin and is thereby alienated from its Creator. But the *Imago Dei,* God's image, although marred, has never been totally destroyed. In fact, that is the only abiding point of contact between the supracultural God in His abiding holiness and culture-bound humanity in its fallen humanness.

Jesus Christ, the Son of God, who was "born in the likeness of man," thereby identifying Himself with humanity, has become the Mediator between God and humankind. By His death on the cross and the resurrection from the dead He is the Savior and Lord of all who trust and confess Him as such. Those who thus trust and confess are transformed by the power of the Holy Spirit. They are reconciled with God, are born anew, have entered a new relationship, and are empowered to do His will in the world.

Confession in Second-Generation Christians

A phenomenal dilemma emerges when the focus on experiential conversion in the first generation shifts to a recital of a confession in the second-, third-, or fourth-generation. The former must be caught and experienced; the latter can be learned and expressed. The one applies predominantly to adults joining the church from without, subsequent to their conversion experience; the other applies more to their children who grow up in a Christian atmosphere or community, joining the church from within the group (Loewen, 1969:5).

"But there are unavoidable dangers in this necessary progress from living *in* an experience to teaching *about* the experience" (Wiens, 1965:5). One is that of imagining that the *form* of one's own experience is the only legitimate *norm* for the experience of others. Furthermore, there is the danger of understanding the subjective as well as the objective facts of one's experience as the only legitimate interpretation for all conversions. The question then arises whether conversion of a middle-aged person, who has for many years lived in the real world of sin, means the same as a conversion of a teenager, who has grown up in and known only the sheltered atmosphere of a Christian home. Both say they are converted. And, of course, they can and may be.

The danger is for the adults to expect of the young person the same kind of experience they have had and for the youth to talk about the same kind of experience he hears his parents or grandparents talk about. Surprisingly, the vocabulary is very similar for both. In the one case it may be authentic, in the other, imitative of expected norms expressed in verbal forms.

The difference, however, may be much greater than the surface evidences. To first-generation Christians—be they from a traditionally pagan or from a neopagan environment—conversion means a dramatic change of lifestyle, attitude, being, and action; it also means faith that trusts God whom the converts meet in personal confrontation when they appropriate His forgiving love; it may also mean the description of the conversion that can be expressed in terms of both the subjective experience as well as in objective doctrinal statements.

The subtlety is that these statements can be taught, but the experience cannot. It is true the Holy Spirit can use even a dogma—and, indeed, He often does, as Freytag (1961:248-53) has reminded us—and thereby brings about genuine conversions in the lives of people. But dogmas and creeds can also be learned and confessed—as indeed they often are thus confessed in second-generation nominal Christianity—as Buehler (1973:106) has shown.

Whenever Christian faith becomes institutionalized it can

either be expressed in good works or it becomes an external, verbal confession of a creed without an internal, experiential dimension. Or again, as Wiens puts it (1965:5), "*faith* comes to mean, not *trust*, but *belief*, that is, the mental acceptance of the truth of the sets of descriptions. But belief and trust are two quite different things." The one is rooted in a belief system, a creed, a dogma, and can be learned, mentally accepted, and verbally recited or confessed, like a confession of faith; the other is rooted in experience, existential living, discipleship, and finds expression in relationships with, and reliance on, God.

Faith in the sense of belief may be acquired as a result of exposure to a creedal system without any or only minor changes of lifestyle; faith in the sense of trust is the accompanying phenomenon of a genuine conversion experience involving a change of ethics and values, loyalty and lordship.

Summary
If Christianity as discipleship under the lordship of Christ were simply a system of creedal statements, a code of ethics, or a set of social mores—all of which can be learned, recited, and adhered to—it would be quite a simple way for second-generation followers to excel in and achieve. But Christianity is more than that. It is a life of relationships, demanding decisions for and commitment to Jesus Christ, Savior and Lord. The challenge of each generation, then, is to decide for itself to make that commitment.

One of the greatest dangers for second-generation Christians is that of a nominal commitment, namely the tendency to confess a creed, water down the ethical norms, follow certain pious practices, and apply the letter of the law rather than live a life governed by the spirit of Christ in relationship with God and others. If no personal commitment to Christ is made by members of each generation, the road leads inevitably to neopaganism which, in fact, is the old paganism in the garb of three or four generations later—or whatever time it takes to complete the cycle.

In essence, Christian conversion is as much for second- or third-generation nominal Christians as for first generation believers converted from paganism, though the type of the experience may vary. In each case, however, people must be born from above in order to become first-generation children of God. Christian conversion cannot be inherited. God has neither grandchildren nor great-grandchildren.

PART IV
Church and Convert: Reciprocity and Responsibility

Chapter 9

Conversion and the Believers' Church

The man who is in Christ must be increasingly Christlike.
                                        —*William Barclay*, 1972.

What is the nature of the believers' church? What are the tasks and responsibilities of the believers' church in view of her mandate from the Lord on the one hand, and the world she lives in on the other? If she carries out her mandate of the ministry of reconciliation and preaches for a verdict so that people do, indeed, become converted, what implications might this have for both the church and the convert? What reciprocal responsibilities emerge as a result for the convert and the church? These and other questions deserve a brief response in this and the final chapter.

Distinctives of the Believers' Church

In 1944 when the crevices of the *kosmos* were still struggling to absorb the life-flow of the masses of the nations' choicest men fallen on the battlefields of global conflict, isolated voices were heard to speak about *Nachfolge* or discipleship. They spoke of love, peace, nonresistance, reconciliation, obedience to Christ, cross-bearing, a separated life, holiness, and full yieldedness to the lordship of Christ. Such is the nature of discipleship. That concept of discipleship describes more accurately than any other the very essence of the believers' church.

Stimulated by an essay by J. Lawrence Burkholder (1962:135-51), I am suggesting five marks that identify the believers' church. Such a church becomes a powerful spiritual entity in the Fourth World, seeking women and men to be converted to Christ, who in turn become responsible members of the church by serving God and others.

Voluntary and Free

Someone has said, "Christians who earnestly love the Word find each other and join together" (Durnbaugh, 1968:4). This is what Martin Luther wanted. As the "third order" of church people he wanted to make provision for those who earnestly desire to be Christians (Luther, 1526:64). His dilemma, however, was that he did not have the people and thus chose to stand with the masses in the territorial church (Bainton, 1950:311).

The voluntary and free church, as understood here, consists of believing members who have joined themselves together without any type of coercion for the purpose of carrying out the biblical mandate in the world. These are believers who have experienced conversion to Christ as a change of life and loyalty; who share a common confession to Christ as Savior and Lord; who have out of their own free will and decision accepted believer's baptism as an essential step in their spiritual pilgrimage to church membership. They have not been *brought by someone else* to the ritual of baptism, but have *themselves come* to be baptized within the fellowship of the free church of believers (cf. Kuen, 1975:141).

Obedience to the Biblical Mandate

In his book on the *Origins of Sectarian Protestantism,* professor Franklin Littel (1973:110) characterizes the radical disciples of the sixteenth-century Reformation as being obedient to the evangelistic mandate. "No words of the Master were given more serious attention by His Anabaptist followers than the Great Commission":

> Go therefore and make disciples of all the nations, baptizing them in the name of the Father and the Son and the Holy Spirit, teaching them to observe all that I commanded you; and lo, I am with you always, even to the end of the age (Matthew 28:19-20, NASB).

The members of the believers' church know Christ as both Redeemer and Master, as reconciling Savior and sending Lord. They know that the apostolate has not ended with the apostolic era. They are not only aware of being *called* to follow the Master, but also of being *sent* as servants with the ministry of reconciliation in a broken world. The call to discipleship has deep theological and ethical consequences, appealing to the will more than to the intellect, for obedience is a matter of the will, not of the mind.

To obey the evangelistic mandate means to take seriously the apostolate of which Arthur Glasser of the School of World Mission, Hans Küng of the University of Tübingen (1967:344 ff.), and Georg Vicedom, Neuendettelsau (1960:46-67) so frequently speak in their preaching and writings. Disciples and apostles, or followers of Christ and missionaries to whom the evangelistic mandate means obedience to Christ, place little emphasis on the sacramental and liturgical aspect of the church; rather, they emphasize the dynamic witness in the power of the Spirit of God, voluntary fellowship in commitment to Christ and to each other, and corporate service to the whole man in a broken world (cf. Yoder, 1972:115).

Obedience to the biblical mandate *in toto* means involvement with men and women, in order to meet their total needs and bring the gospel of Christ to them with the purpose of leading them to an encounter with Christ who makes people whole.

Love and Peace Witness

This is the second major characteristic of the believers' church (Burkholder, 1962:143). The only "sword" the disciples of Christ know is the "sword of the Spirit, which is the word of God" (Ephesians 6:17). The use of that sword, Paul leads us to believe, is the most effective weapon to conquer the world and bring men and women to discipleship under the lordship of Christ. That sword in the hands of the disciples functions as "the power of God for salvation" (Romans 1:16). In fact, it is the message of reconciliation, as we have shown above, that leads to faith, healing, forgiveness, conversion, believer's baptism; yea, it leads to being a new creature in Christ. When the messengers of peace and love proclaim that word, those who believe cannot resist its force. No wonder then that Isaiah was prompted to say,

> How lovely on the mountains
> Are the feet of him who brings good news,
> Who announces peace
> And brings good news of happiness,
> Who announces salvation,
> And says to Zion, "your God reigns!"   (Isaiah 52:7)

The members of the kingdom of God maintain and foster a new attitude to spiritual and social needs, justice and equality, property and poverty, neighborhoods and neighborliness. They are governed by the rules of the kingdom here and now. They are motivated to a lifestyle that comes as close to the ethical and spiritual standards outlined by the teachings of Jesus (e.g., the Sermon on the Mount) and the apostles as is possible in this life. Harold S. Bender characterized the church rather fittingly when he wrote:

> The "new people" of God are ... under the new covenant and order with a new mode of organization and administration, a new standard of ethics, a new relationship to the world, and new resources in Christ and the Holy Spirit for their life under the lordship of Christ (Bender, 1962:4).

Willingness to Bear the Cross

We hear the words of our Savior and Lord saying, "If anyone wishes to come after Me, let him deny himself, and take up his cross daily, and follow Me" (Luke 9:23, NASB). As a member of the people of God, the disciple is always a cross-bearer.

The manifestation of this characteristic of the believers' church comes to the fore in the struggle between the two realms—on the one hand the realm of the kingdom of God, and on the other hand the realm of the kingdom of this world. The central event in this struggle is the death of Christ. Those who step into and remain in the *imitatio Christi* (imitation of Christ) have, in effect, stepped into the arena of faith. It is always in the sign of the cross of Christ under which they understand both the nature of their faith and their fate.

Burkholder (1962:146) maintains that the people of God have a history of suffering from the very beginning and will continue in that spirit until "the apocalyptic events of the latter days. In this struggle truth is vindicated. It will be finally victorious." When the church is faithful to its calling to be a *witnessing* church *to* the world, it will always be a *martyr* church *in* the world.

A cross-bearing church is characterized by obedience to the cross-bearing Lord. Such obedience is that of a "martyr-witness," "disregarding all risks, accepting all consequences," as the late Kenneth Strachan has reminded us (1968:69). The way of discipleship is a way of "becoming obedient to the point of death, even death on a cross" (Philippians 2:8, NASB).

A Life of Separation and Holiness

Burkholder has said, "If Luther rediscovered the biblical doctrine of faith, the Anabaptists rediscovered the biblical call to holiness" (1962:148). Whenever people of God have demonstrated a high quality of moral and spiritual life, the church has also grown most rapidly in quantitative terms. The records of such movements as the early church, the Anabaptists, and the Great Awakenings serve to illustrate that claim.

If we desire the church of Jesus Christ to bring lost people to discipleship under Christ's lordship through a genuine conversion experience, we must not water down Christian living, but emphasize the "cost of discipleship," to use Bonhoeffers' words. The theme of the Bible about the lifestyle of God's people in the kingdom of God confronts us with such realities as repentance and confession, righteousness and rightness, love and peace, brotherhood and brotherliness, sacrifice and hospitality, triumphant faith and eschatological hope.

To *be* converted means to *live* converted; it means being in the world, but not of it. The problem is all too often that the people who call themselves by Christ's name blend so well with the unconverted people of the Fourth World that they see no distinction between themselves and the Christians.

The concept of separation and holy living emanates from a high view of the holiness of God. Our mission as disciples of Jesus Christ is not only to call people to repent and become converted; we are also called to discipline each other as converts and to live under the absolute authority of Jesus Christ who calls His people to "holiness unto the Lord."

The Priesthood of All Believers

The apostles formulated the principle: "You are a . . . royal priesthood" (1 Peter 2:9) because Christ has gathered the believers into His kingdom and made them "priests of God his Father" (Revelation 1:6). The medieval church exchanged this uniquely inclusive characteristic of believers in favor of an exclusive clerical priesthood. It took the scriptural insight of the Reformers of the sixteenth century to recover that lost principle once again. Thus Martin Luther could write to the "German nobility" that all believers are equal in their spiritual standing before God and all have been dedicated to be priests through baptism (cf. Kuen, 1975:219).

Unfortunately, Luther and the other Reformers were unable to carry out the New Testament idea of the priesthood of all believers. The conditions of the priestly character of the believers are conversion and living faith. In the context of the territorial state church in which all are baptized—regardless of a faith commitment—those conditions need not be met. Thus the Protestant church theoretically formulated the concept of the priesthood of all believers but failed to carry it out in practice. The Church of the Reformers, as Emil Brunner has pointed out, remained explicitly a clerical church. And that for good reasons: those who were not converted to be children and people of God could not be priests of God (Kuen, 1975:220).

The principle of the priesthood of all believers was put into practice by the Anabaptists. What the "Magisterial Reformers" originally envisioned about the believers' church, the "Radical Reformers" (Williams, 1975:302; Durnbaugh, 1968:64) carried to its existential consequences. What Luther called the "dritte Art," or third kind of church, is composed of those "who want to be Christians in earnest." Since he did not have that kind of people in the *corpus Christianum*, he stated that he neither could nor desired "to begin such a congregation or assembly or make rules for it" (Luther, 1526:64). John Calvin had similar thoughts on the church. What he called the *tertier nota*, the third mark of the church, was a church of believers who were all one in "obedience, brotherhood-love, suffering, and discipline" (Littell, 1961:27-28).

Like Luther, Calvin was unable to translate the concept of the priesthood of all believers into practice. The Anabaptists on the other hand actualized what the mainstream Reformers conceptualized. The Anabaptists conceived of the church not as consisting of the inclusive *corpus christianum* in the "Constantinian-Theodosian" tradition (Brunner, 1953:104), but the exclusive *Corpus Christi*, the body of Christ as "one priestly nation" without any distinction between the lay people in the pews and the ordained preachers behind the pulpit (cf. Friedmann, 1973:120).

Conversion as Primary Concern

"To what extent is it necessary, or desirable, for the Christian church to work for the conversion of the non-Christian to Christianity"? This question by professor Eric Sharpe (1969:221) of the University of Manchester would have been unthinkable a few decades ago. But not so today.

The Validity of Conversion Questioned

In an age when far-reaching changes have come upon the Christian church, people from some quarters look at preaching for conversion as a matter of proselytizing. Thus, in certain quarters of contemporary mission theology, the validity of conversion has become an issue of debate. Some go so far as to say that "the responsibility and goal of mission work is no longer that of converting unbelievers, but rather that of partnership in building up the Third World" (quoted in *Lebendige Gemeinde*, 1973, page 23). Even such a well-known book as *The Theology of the Christian Mission* with more than two dozen contributors makes only two or three incidental references to conversion (Anderson, 1961:75, 132). This may indicate that many mission theologians prefer to shun the controversial issue. Paul Löffler (1969:7) very perceptively says that the conversion question "has proved to be one of the most obstinate in the history of the ecumenical movement."

What Löffler means is evidenced by Ronan R. Hoffman in his article, "Conversion and the Mission of the Church," which appeared in the 1968 winter issue of the *Journal of Ecumenical Studies*. Hoffman states that in Catholic circles the emphasis has shifted from conversion to propagation. In more general terms he asserts that "conversion of all mankind to Christianity through missions was the church's aim" in the past, but "contemporary Christians no longer accept this notion" (Hoffman, 1968:1-2). In accord with much of ecumenical and conciliatory thinking, Hoffman believes that all religions, including Christianity, must carry on dialogue "in an atmosphere of mutual esteem and respect," and let "all the peoples walk each in the name of its god" just as Christians "walk in the name of the Lord—God, Jesus Christ—for ever and ever." Christian witness and service should continue, but not "proselytizing and conversion," Hoffman implies (1968:19).

Priority of Conversion Preaching

The biblical position is different from that stated above. God has never changed his demand that people turn to Him and be saved. The people of God or the believers' church accept the biblical mandate *in toto* and understand the Great Commission as placing priority on discipling the nations, which means to bring about conversion in a spiritual sense, and not in the sense of social change only. Surely the church must engage in social action. That is an integral part of the biblical mandate and a test of the church's commitment to Christ. The church must bring "the whole gospel to the whole man," as professor Victor Adrian of Toronto has stated (1971:4). When the basic human problem of alienation from God through sin is solved and people are reconciled with God and others, social change is inevitable. Yet Eric Sharpe rightly insists that "the church must work for the conversion of the non-Christians. The gospel must be preached to the whole world; disciples must be made of every nation" (1969:221). "For the Protestant Missionary Movement we can prove," asserts Löffler, "that the conversion of individuals or groups has been the stated goal from its inception at the end of the 18th century" (1968:7).

The Church's Mission and Conversion

Dr. Löffler points out that the most convincing arguments for the "validity of the Christian Mission" (Trueblood, 1972:title) are set forth by Gustav Warneck, who in his day was the recognized spokesman for and exponent of the mission of the church and the preaching of the gospel for a verdict. In his monumental five-volume *Evangelische Mis-*

sionslehre (1892-1905) and scores of other books, essays, and articles written between 1868 and 1910, Warneck systematically presents the biblical, theological, ethical, historical, ethnical, and ecclesiological case for the Christian church in mission and the priority of preaching the gospel of the kingdom of God to bring about conversion. Within the framework of this study I can only refer to Warneck's work and translate a few excerpts to make my point.

In addition to his most extensive exegetical study of the biblical mandate as presented in the Synoptic Gospels, Warneck (1874:41-392, passim) also deals with Paul's understanding of conversion (1897:240-59). Elsewhere Warneck summarizes Paul's position on conversion, a position which the "apostle to the Gentiles" traces back to his own call from God (Acts 9:15; 21:18). That position, according to Warneck, is

> to carry Christ's name to the Gentiles and to open their eyes so that they might be converted from darkness to light and from the power of Satan to God, in order to receive forgiveness of sins and a heritage together with those who are sanctified through faith in Christ (1902:178).

From the teachings of Jesus and Paul, Warneck concludes, conversion of all peoples should result from preaching the gospel of repentance and the gospel of the kingdom of God. He writes:

> The task of mission is nothing else than to extend the Kingdom of God across the entire globe, which means teaching about the Kingdom, calling people into the Kingdom, gather, nurture, and keep those who belong to its community. The purpose of the Kingdom is to encompass the total life of mankind and to penetrate all its associations, structures, and institutions. Because it spreads from the inside to the outside it must first of

all be planted in the hearts of men and begin with their renewal. The power opposing the Kingdom on every hand is sin with its sting of death. But the power which overcomes this enemy is the Saviour of Sinners with His gift of life. To bring about redemption from the super-power of darkness, transference into the Kingdom of Jesus Christ, conversion from dead idols to the living God and a new walk in obedience of faith—all that was at the very heart of the apostolic task—must remain the center of the missionary task in our day (Warneck, 1902:179).

Although Warneck acknowledges the total need of the whole person, he insists that the primary task of the church and her mission must focus on making disciples (1902:211 f.) which includes conversion, the turning away from sin toward living for God (1902:217).

Conversion and Church Membership

If the unregenerate cannot enter the kingdom of God, as the Bible indeed teaches, and if the kingdom of God is a present as well as a future reality, then the church has only two options: it can either discontinue preaching the message of the kingdom of God and cease to be the church of Jesus Christ; or it can continue preaching the gospel of the kingdom by calling people everywhere to be reconciled to God and live a life of discipleship under the lordship of Jesus Christ and be the visible believers' church in the world. The German missiologist Georg Vicedom quotes Löffler as saying that the church exists to carry out God's mandate. He points out what happens when it fails in its primary task.

Fellowship without a passion for conversion of men leads to a ghetto-existence; service without the call to conversion is a mere gesture without hope; Christian instruction without conversion is mere religiosity without a verdict; dialog without a challenge to conversion remains fruitless verbosity (Vicedom, 1969:72).

Whenever the church is truly the church of Jesus Christ it will lead multitudes to conversion and baptism and will integrate them into the community of believers for worship, fellowship, instruction, and edification (Acts 2:41-47). The convert, in turn, becomes the disciple under the lordship of Christ.

According to each one's spiritual gifts (1 Corinthians 12:1, 4-7), the new convert will be the new *marturos* or witness, the energetic *euaggelistes* or evangelist, the ever-sent *apostolos* or missionary of the church in order to lead nonbelievers from the unevangelized Fourth World everywhere to a conversion experience, to subsequent discipleship of the people of God and membership in the believers' church.

To conclude, I borrow the final words from professor Elton Trueblood's book, *The Company of the Committed,* saying, "If God, as we believe, is truly revealed in the life of Christ, the most important thing to Him is the creation of centers of loving fellowship, which in turn infect the world. Whether the world can be redeemed in this way we do not know, but it is at least clear that there is no other way" (1961:113).

Chapter 10

The New Convert and the Church

God wants all men everywhere to be saved and become responsible members of His church.

—*Donald A. McGavran,* 1973.

In a theological discourse on the church and her mission, Otto Michel, a contemporary of Bonhoeffer, wrote in "Gottesherrschaft und Völkerwelt" that conversion in the biblical context has a unique meaning and always leads to unique relationships and unique ways of responsible expression.

By "return" the Bible means a turning that proceeds from the very depth of the heart of helpless men toward the helping God. Can the call of God's grace demand a different answer from man than that of total return? Grace on the one hand and return on the other are placed on the same relational axis to one another. The uniqueness of conversion in the Bible leads to the new insight that the convert cannot remain by himself in isolation; it always leads to incorporation in a new covenantal fellowship, namely the fellowship of the community of the converted.

The act of returning leads to the church of the returned ones; it provides for man a new prayer and a new kind of service to

God, a new brotherhood and a new kind of service to fellowmen (Michel, 1941:226, translation mine).

These words by professor Michel are indicative of the relationship between the convert and the church.

Conversion and the Implications for the Convert

The primary human problem is neither social nor physical, but spiritual and moral. Sin has separated, alienated, and estranged us from God, the creature from the Creator. In the conversion process sin is forgiven, the gulf of separation bridged, a new relationship established, and life transformed. Christ has become Lord, the Controller. Alienation and isolation are ended. A new relationship has been established.

Ever since creation, humankind has borne the *Imago Dei* in its very being. Sin, however, has marred that divine image and caused human life to become fragmented, broken up, separated from life in God. In fact, we have experienced spiritual death. "This death is separation from full existence, and is answered by a spiritual birth, by the resurrection power of Christ giving new life" (Augsburger, 1970:90). As the Holy Spirit performs the new birth (John 3:3-8), the human spirit responds and realizes that it has been renewed, quickened, made whole. Fragmentation and brokenness are ended. Wholeness has been restored.

The converted can now confess that not only their spirit has become alive again (Romans 8:10), but also that God's Spirit dwells in them (Romans 8:11). There is a new Presence in life, namely the Spirit of God who communicates to the spirit of the convert that he, the convert, is a child of God (Romans 8:16). When the lordship of Christ and discipleship in the Spirit meet, then true "discipling" is taking place. The new presence of the Holy Spirit is a creative presence. The convert becomes an instrument "unto good works" (Ephesians 2:10). It is also a directive and normative presence, enabling the convert to live by the new ethical and moral standards under the lordship of Christ (cf. Augsburger, 1970:92). Perversion and selfishness are ended. The Holy Spirit has become the Guide. Christ has become the Lord. The convert has become a disciple, a learner, and follower of Christ the Lord.

As the new convert walks in newness of life, he is in the process of becoming "more like the Master." This process has opened up new vistas, new possibilities, new privileges. The convert has once again gained freedom (Romans 8:2) to become more and more transformed into the image of the Son of God (Ephesians 4:13) and thereby reflecting in increasing measure the *Imago Dei*. Indifference toward God and bondage in sin are ended. Concern to abide in His will has gained priority. The newly gained freedom is linked to a new sense of responsibility commensurate with discipleship under the Lord Christ.

Another implication is a sense of purpose and direction. The natural person in the Fourth World lives a life of meaninglessness. His values are measured in terms of fleeting relative standards. He lacks sense of purpose and, as a consequence, experiences futility and despair. In the life of the new convert, however, all this has been transformed. Meaninglessness and futility are ended. There is now purpose, direction, and abundance in life and service. That is not to say that there are no problems. But the disciple always knows who his Master is. A disciple never carries his cross alone.

Finally, conversion implies new ethical standards and good works. According to Acts 26:20, God's demand is not only that people repent, but also that they perform deeds which are appropriate to repentance. Professor William Barclay of the University of Glasgow makes a very pertinent observation when he asserts:

> It cannot be too often said that, although the New Testament never says that a man can be saved *by* works, it always insists that a man is saved *for* works; and any conversion which does not produce a moral and ethical effect upon a man's life and character is not a real conversion at all. . . . A new chastity, a new purity, a new beauty, a new quality of caring must be an essential part of the result of any conversion experience (Barclay, 1972:60-61).

What Barclay has said is a contemporary affirmation of the Apostle James' invective against a faith-alone Christianity without ethical and social responsibility. When James spoke about the indispensability of a demonstration of faith in the life of the new convert, he sought to "illustrate the gospel's full meaning by showing the relationship of works to faith, and deeds to words," as Sherwood E. Wirt asserts in his *Social Conscience of the Evangelical* (1968:15).

The Responsibility of the Church

Whether the church exists on old ground or is planted on virgin soil, the new convert must be incorporated into and become a vital part of the local body of believers. From the New Testament context it appears that the church assumed a responsibility for the converts to nourish them in their newfound life in Christ. Several dimensions are to be noted.

The Sociological Dimension

There is the socioreligious responsibility of acceptance. Even before the convert is baptized, the church must demonstrate her full acceptance of the convert into friendship and fellowship. This becomes particularly crucial in cultures with strong kinship bonds and social cohesiveness. Although social dislocation should be minimized at all costs, the young convert must find "a place to feel at home" in the circle of believers where people love each other and care for one another.

When a young lad was asked why he walked for miles to attend D. L. Moody's Sunday school class, he replied, "They love a fellow over there." Christian love is the test of discipleship, as Christ tells us in John 13:35. The Catholic song so popular among today's Christian youth is quite correct: "And they'll know we are Christians by our love."

The Ritual Dimension

There are two religious rites which the believers' church is bound to observe together with, and administer to, the young convert—believer's baptism and the Lord's Supper. Whatever the interpretation of these rites may be, they must be accepted as spiritual givens "because they go back to the institution of Jesus Himself" (Brunner, 1953:67). The New Testament makes the significant point that the very genesis of the church lies in the administration of baptism to the young converts and in the participation of baptized believers in the Lord's Supper (Acts 2:38-42).

A. Baptism and the Supper in the Ongoing Church

In his stimulating book on *The Misunderstanding of the Church,* Emil Brunner offers a pertinent commentary on the meaning of baptism and the meal of bread and wine for the ongoing church.

> Through these two rites the individual is joined to the real and concrete congregation of the faithful in such a way as could not happen—at least not so unmistakably—through the mere

word of preaching. One can listen to the announcement of the divine Word without belonging to the community, without identifying oneself with it, abiding in it, and taking part in its life. The so-called sacraments are the *verbum communale*, the form of the Word through which the individual is really incorporated and made one with the community. The complementary aspect as it were of the same matter is that through these rites there finds expression the truth that the fellowship of Jesus is grounded in an *action* of God, which takes place in the real historical world, and for the completion of which God uses the Christian community. The sacrament is the *verbum activum*. The communion of Christ is realized through a common action of the congregation, and is realized in the congregation. To this corresponds the historical fact that it was the so-called sacraments which gradually, more than anything else, erected a breakwater against the tide of individualistic enthusiasm and so held the community together as a community (Brunner, 1953:67-68).

B. The Young Convert and Baptism

I have already made reference to the significance of believer's baptism (Chapter 5 above) as it touches the theological concern in conversion. The emphasis here is on baptism as it touches the young convert and his relationship to the church.

Young converts—particularly college and university students—frequently raise the question whether or not baptism should follow conversion. Their concern is not so much with the mode of baptism as with the validity of the rite itself following the conversion experience. Similarly, converts in nominal church settings often ask whether they should be "rebaptized" if they have been baptized as infants or unconverted adults.

In response to these questions it is imperative to stress the fact that we are here dealing with believer's baptism which means water baptism subsequent to conversion and a faith commitment to Christ as Savior and Lord. Furthermore, it should be pointed out that baptism may not be absolutely necessary for eternal life. So at least it would appear from the brief conversation between Jesus and the dying thief who had no chance to receive baptism upon his conversion on the cross (Luke 23:40-43). That baptism is not a prerequisite for salvation can be deducted also from the missionary mandate according to Mark. Whereas Matthew records the risen Lord's command to make disciples of all peoples by baptizing them in the name of the Triune God and then to teach the new converts all that Jesus had commanded (Matthew 28:16-20), Mark stresses the preaching of the good news, faith in response to that preaching, and baptism as an essential ingredient for salvation. Then he adds: "But those who refuse to believe will be condemned" (Mark 16:15-16). This would imply that faith, but not baptism, is absolutely necessary for salvation.

When we look at the practice of the apostolic church, we must conclude that believer's baptism was valued very highly. All those who believed in Jesus and were converted were also baptized. On the day of Pentecost thousands of Jewish people listened to the preaching on the death and resurrection of Christ. Three thousand of them responded by repenting of their sins and by receiving or believing the Word of God. Those who believed were also baptized (Acts 2:38-41). Similar incidents where people heard the Word, believed in Jesus, and were baptized are repeated many times in the story of the early church. (Cf. the Samaritans, Acts 8:4-8 and 12; the treasurer of Ethiopia, 8:26-39; Saul of Tarsus, 9:1-18; Cornelius and his household, 10:30-48; the saleswoman Lydia, 16:13-15; the Philippian jailer, 16:29-33.)

C. Baptism and Church Membership

Just as the matter of baptism raises some questions, so also that of church membership raises questions on the part of some young converts: Should I join a local church or should I remain independent? If I join the church, should I first be baptized? Or should I be baptized but not join a local congregation to assume responsibility in it?

There are many denominations and local congregations who administer the rite of believer's baptism to young converts but do not stress church membership. Then there are those who stress church membership, but do not make baptism a prerequisite (cf. Bussemer, 1968:57 ff.; Erdlenbruch and Ritter, 1972:40). Then there are others who maintain that baptism and church membership should follow the conversion experience. Emil Brunner has stated that baptism is the commonly accepted sign for church membership (Kuen, 1975:136) and that the "obedience of faith" (Glaubensgehorsam) is the decisive factor whether or not one belongs to the church (Brunner, 1935:142).

It is the thesis of this study that believer's baptism and church membership are essential steps in the spiritual pilgrimage of the young convert. The record of the Book of Acts confirms the following steps: preaching and hearing of the Word, faith and conversion in response to the message, baptism by, and affiliation with, the church (Acts 2:41; 9:18, 26; 11:26; 16:13-15, 40).

Conversion alone is insufficient for giving full expression to the life of discipleship which is best expressed in the believer's church (Schmitz and Wöhrle, 1968:74).

D. Church Membership and the Lord's Supper

One of the richest experiences inside the church is the participation in the Lord's Supper. The European Bible

teacher Alfred Kuen stresses the importance of the Lord's
Supper to the believing and baptized church member. Upon
an extensive exegetical study of the question, Kuen concludes that the primitive church observed a simple, logical
order in the events of the Christian's life and his relationship
to the church's symbolic rites:

> Whoever had had an encounter with the Word of God and
> followed the Lord's call to repentance and faith had expe-
> rienced conversion and regeneration. He was subsequently
> baptized and received into the *ekklesia*, the congregation of
> those who likewise had obeyed God's call. He was then admit-
> ted to participate in the Lord's Supper. Every difficulty that has
> in the course of history arisen in the developing church can be
> traced back to the fact that this God-given order has been
> violated (Kuen, 1975:142, translation mine).

The Lord's Supper has many meanings. Two of them
stand out above all others: one leads the participant to reflect
on the past, the other to look ahead to the future. Both,
however, center in the Person of Christ. In retrospect the
Supper is a vivid reminder of our redemption. When the Israelites participated in the Passover meal they reflected on
the great work of redemption Yahweh had brought about by
saving them from slavery in Egypt; when the Christians
partake of the Lord's Supper they are reminded of their
conversion from a life of sin and darkness to a life of freedom
and light.

Paul reminds us in 1 Corinthians 5:7 that Christ, God's
Passover Lamb, has been slain for us. Each time we share
the Lord's table with other believers we are, in fact, pro-
claiming—not in words, but in action—that the Lamb of
God took away our sin. The symbols of bread and wine re-
mind us of His broken body and shed blood.

The Lord's Supper also has eschatological significance. The Apostle Paul reminds the Corinthian believers that they are to remember the Lord's death every time they "eat this bread and drink the cup . . . until he comes" (1 Corinthians 11:26). Thus the young convert has come in possession of two immovable pillars of truth when he partakes of the Lord's Supper: when he looks back he sees in faith the pillar of Christ's death on the cross for his sins; when he looks forward he sees in hope the pillar of the Lord's return for his eternal redemption.

The Didactic Dimension

Christ commanded that the discipling process must include instruction. The early church leaders took this didactic dimension very seriously (cf. Acts 4:5 f.; 5:28) and taught "in Jesus the resurrection from the dead" (Acts 4:2). The first missionaries went from house to house, from city to city, teaching the Word to the young converts (cf. Acts 11:26; 15:35; 20:20; 28:31). The teachable convert can thus grow in Christ by the teaching ministry of the church. The young convert must have a *didaskalos*, a teacher, and himself become a true *mathetes*, a disciple or learner. As he learns and grows in Christian knowledge, he himself is a potential teacher to others, depending on whether or not he has been endowed with the spiritual gift of teaching.

The didactic dimension has a stabilizing effect on the convert. It is again the Apostle Paul with his companions who went through all the regions of Asia Minor, "strengthening all the disciples" (Acts 18:23). The missionary, the evangelist, or whoever may have been the advocate of the gospel should make provision for discipling in the sense of providing the convert with the means of Christian growth and maturation.

The Existential Dimension

The whole matter of church discipline is too big a topic to enter into within the context of this study. As I have shown elsewhere (Kasdorf, 1970:40 f.), there are at least five phases in the process of disciplining the offending fellow-believer. All have to do with the existential dimension of the Christian life. One of these phases is preventative in nature. To preventative church discipline belongs the ministry of comfort, encouragement, and admonition. I have been impressed how frequently the Indonesian Christians speak and write about comforting one another. We in the West are inclined to confine that ministry to times of intense emotional and spiritual stress caused by a variety of experiences a person may have, including loss of property, self-confidence, or loved ones. Where comfort comes to a person at the right time, he may find the moral and spiritual strength to cope effectively with the problems and be prevented from severer disappointments.

Another aspect is encouragement. Paul visited the young churches in Macedonia, giving "them much encouragement" (Acts 20:2). I recall with gratitude the encouragement I received as a young convert from older brothers in the faith. "He who enters the church has a right to look for encouragement in the Christian way" (Barclay, 1972:87), whether that encouragement be needed in a time of new adventure along the way of the young spiritual pilgrim or in times of tests and trials, or even in times of shame and failure. The community of believers is a community of mutual care and encouragement. The hand of the believer should be stretched out as much to aid a feeble brother in need of a friend, as to the unconverted in the Fourth World.

Finally, there is the responsibility of admonition. Luke records a moving incident in which Paul reminds the

Ephesian elders how he has not ceased for three years to admonish every one of them day and night with tears (Acts 20:31). The ministry of admonition is not the easiest, yet it is one of the most effective forms of a preventative approach to more severe measures of church discipline (Kasdorf, 1970:40-46). (For an excellent treatment on church discipline, see Jeschke, 1972.)

Conclusion

The life of the new convert becomes most meaningful when responsibilities are reciprocated. Thus he shares in the corporate mission of the people of God. Although conversion is personal, it is never individualistic; it may be well described as the "end of individualism and the entry into fellowship" (Barclay, 1972:71). It is the young convert's duty to build relationships and actively demonstrate his discipleship through corporate prayer, service, communion, and worship.

As a member of the "Company of the Committed" (Trueblood, 1961) the convert shares both blessings and obligations in "the fellowship of forgiven sinners" (Augsburger, 1964:61). As a "forgiven sinner" he has become a "saint" (cf. Romans 1:7; Colossians 1:2; Philippians 1:1). He no longer conforms to the norms of the world, but to the rule of Christ, Savior and Lord.

Sources Cited

Adams, Bob E.
1973 "La Conversion," *Diálogo Teológico*. No. 1:83

Adrian, Victor
1971 "The Whole Gospel to the Whole Man." A Study Conference Paper on the Relationship of Proclamation to Social Action. *The Christian Leader*. Dec. 14: 4-9.

Ahrens, Th.
1975 "Theologische Stimmen," *Zeitschrift für Mission*. 1, No. 3:180-185.

Anderson, Gerald (ed.)
1961 *A Theology of the Christian Mission*. New York and Nashville: Abingdon Press.

Arndt, William F., and F. Wilbur Gingrich
1952 *Greek-English Lexicon of the New Testament and Other Early Christian Literature*, 4th ed. Chicago: University of Chicago Press.

Arza, Zelada de
1976 "En tu Palavra Señor, encontré el verdadero camino," *La Voz del Rebaño*. 4, No. 15:5.

Augsburger, Myron S.
1961 *Quench Not the Spirit*. Scottdale: Herald Press.

1964 *Invitation to Discipleship*. Scottdale: Herald Press.

1970 "Modern Man and the New Man," in *Consultation on Anabaptist Mennonite Theology*. Edited by A. J. Klassen. Fresno, Calif.: Council of Mennonite Seminaries, pp. 78-79.

Bainton, Roland

1950 *Here I Stand*. A Life of Martin Luther. Nashville and New York: Abingdon.

Bamberger, Otto

1956 *Was ist es um Sünde und Erbsünde?* Witten (Ruhr): Bundes-Verlag.

Barclay, William

1959 *The Daily Study Bible. The Letters to the Galatians and Ephesians*. Edinburgh: Saint Andrew Press.

1972 *Turning to God*. Grand Rapids: Baker Book House.

Barnett, Homer G.

1953 *Innovation: The Basis of Cultural Change*. New York: McGraw Hill.

Barth, Christoph

1967 "Notes on 'Return' in the Old Testament," *The Ecumenical Review*. 19:310-312.

Bender, Harold S.

1944 "The Anabaptist Vision," *Church History*. 13:3-24.

1962 *These Are My People*. The New Testament Church. Scottdale: Herald Press.

Beyerhaus, Peter

1964 "The Three Selves Formula," *International Review of Missions*. 53:393-407.

Bittlinger, Arnold

1967 *Gifts and Graces*. A Commentary on 1 Corinthians 12-14. Translated by Herbert Klassen, supervised by Michael Harper. Grand Rapids: William B. Eerdmans.

Blanke, Fritz

1961 *Brothers in Christ*. Scottdale: Herald Press.

Blaser, Klauspeter

1974 "Kommunikation des Evangeliums—Evangelium der

Kommunikation," *Evangelisches Missions Magazin*. 118, No. 3:105-121.

Blauw, Johannes

1974 *The Missionary Nature of the Church*. A Survey of Biblical Theology of Mission. Grand Rapids: Eerdmans.

Bloesch, Donald G.

1968 *The Crisis of Piety*. Essays Toward a Theology of the Christian Life. Grand Rapids: Eerdmans.

Bonhoeffer, Dietrich

1954 *Life Together*. Translated and with an Introduction by John Doberstein. New York: Harper and Row.

1961 *The Cost of Discipleship*. Revised and unabridged edition. Translated by R. H. Fuller from the German *Nachfolge* of 1937. New York: Macmillan.

Brunner, Emil

1935 *Unser Glaube*. Bern: Gotthelf-Verlag.

1947 *The Divine Imperative*. A Study in Christian Ethics. Translated by Olive Wyon. Philadelphia: Westminster Press.

1953 *The Misunderstanding of the Church*. Translated by Harold Knight. Philadelphia: The Westminster Press.

Burkholder, J. Lawrence

1962 "The Anabaptist Vision of Discipleship," in *The Recovery of the Anabaptist Vision*. Edited by Guy F. Hershberger. Scottdale: Herald Press, pp. 135-151.

Bussemer, Konrad

1968 *Die Gemeinde Jesu Christi*. 6th ed. Witten (Ruhr): Bundes-Verlag.

Chambers, Oswald

1945 *My Utmost for His Highest*. New York: Dodd, Mead and Co.

Clark, Walter Houston

1965 "William James: Contributions to the Psychology of Religious Conversion," *Pastoral Psychology*. 16:29-36.

Costas, Orlando E.

1974 *The Church and Its Mission: A Shattering Critique*

from the Third World. Wheaton: Tyndale House Press.

Cotterell, F. Peter

 1974 "The Conversion Crux," *Missiology.* 2:183-190.

De Dietrich, Suzanne

 1958 *The Witnessing Community.* Philadelphia: Westminster Press.

Delius, Eberhard

 1940 "Zwei Typen pietistischer Verkündigung unter den Heiden," *Evangelische Missionszeitschrift.* 1:259-267.

Durnbaugh, Donald F.

 1968 *The Believers' Church.* New York: The Macmillan Company.

Erdlenbruch, Ernst Wilhelm, und Heinz-Adolf Ritter

 1972 *Freie evangelische Gemeinden.* Witten (Ruhr): Bundes-Verlag.

Fergeson, Earl H.

 1965 "The Definition of Religious Conversion," *Pastoral Psychology.* 17:8-16.

Freytag, Walter

 1932 "Zur Psychologie der Bekehrung bei Primitiven," in *Botschafter an Christi Statt.* Edited by Martin Schlunk. Gütersloh: Evangelischer Verlag "Der Rufer," pp. 281-306.

 1961 *Reden und Aufsätze.* 2 vols. Edited by Jan Hermeling und Hans Jochen Margull. Munich: Christian Kaiser Verlag.

Friedmann, Robert

 1973 *The Theology of Anabaptism.* Scottdale: Herald Press.

Friedrich, Gerhard (ed.)

 1971 Kittel's *Theological Dictionary of the New Testament.* Translated and edited by Geoffrey W. Bromiley. Vol. 7. Grand Rapids: William B. Eerdmans.

Friesen, P. M.

 1911 *Die Alt-Evangelische Mennonitische Brüderschaft in Russland (1789-1910).* Halbstadt, Taurien: Verlagsgesellschaft "Raduga."

Gesangbuch

1955 *Gesangbuch der Mennoniten Brüdergemeinde.* 7th ed. Selected and compiled by the Music Committee of the Canadian Conference of the Mennonite Brethren of North America. Winnipeg: No publisher given.

Glasser, Arthur F.

1973 "Church Growth and Theology," in *God, Man and Church Growth.* Edited by Alan R. Tippett. Grand Rapids: Eerdmans, pp. 52-68.

Godet, Frederick

1956 *Commentary on the Epistle to the Romans.* Translated from the French by A. Cusin (1883). Revised and edited by Talbot Chambers. Grand Rapids: Zondervan.

Goethe, Johann Wolfgang von

1957 *Goethes Werke.* Bd. I (München: Knaur Nachfolger), *Faust I* (Ca. 1780), pp. 721-829.

Graham, Billy

1967 "Conversion—a Personal Revolution," *The Ecumenical Review.* 19:271-284.

Green, Michael

1975 *Evangelism in the Early Church.* Grand Rapids: Eerdmans.

Griffiths, Michael

1972 *Es gibt Grösseres.* Translated by Gerlind Krause. Giessen und Basel: Brunnen Verlag. Original English: *Give Up Your Small Ambitions.* Downers Grove: Inter-Varsity Press, 1970.

Haarbeck, Theodor

1922 *Biblische Glaubenslehre.* 8th ed. Elberfeld: Buchhandlung der Evangelischen Gesellschaft für Deutschland.

Haenchen, Ernst

1971 *The Acts of the Apostles.* A Commentary. Translated from the 14th German edition by Bernard Noble and Gerald Shinn. Revised and updated by R. Mcl. Wilson. Philadelphia: Westminster Press.

Heikkinen, Jacob W.
    1966 "Conversion. A Biblical Study." Unpublished paper.
        (Dittoed.) Excellent.
    1967 "Notes on 'Epistrepho' and 'Metanoeo,'" *The Ecu-
        menical Review.* 19:313-316.
Hiebert, D. Edmund
    1975 Personal letter to the writer, Oct. 20, 1975. (On file.)
Hiebert, Paul G.
    1974 "Conceptual Backgrounds of Conversion." A paper
        presented at the Institute of Mennonite Studies,
        Elkhart, Ind., Mar. 6-8 (Xeroxed)
    1976 *Cultural Anthropology.* Philadelphia: J. B. Lippincott
        Company.
Hoffman, Ronan R.
    1968 "Conversion and the Mission of the Church." *Journal
        of Ecumenical Studies.* 5 (Winter): 1-20.
Hogg, C. F., and W. E. Vine
    1959 *The Epistles to the Thessalonians.* London: Pickering
        and Inglis.
Holladay, William Lee
    1958 *The Root Subh in the Old Testament.* Leiden: E. J.
        Brill.
Humphreys, Fisher
    1976 "An Apologetic Armoury," *The Evangelical Quarterly.*
        44:90-95.
James, William
    1905 *The Varieties of Religious Experience.* London:
        Longmans, Green and Co.
Jellinghaus, Theodor
    1874 "Die Kolhs in Ostindien und ihre Christianisierung,"
        Allgemeine Missions-Zeitschrift. 1 (1874):24-35; 59-71;
        104-112; 167-184; 203-214; 253-270; 341-350.
Jeschke, Marlin
    1972 *Discipling the Brother.* Scottdale: Herald Press.
Jones, E. Stanley
    1959 *Conversion.* New York: Abingdon Press.

Kähler, Martin

1893 "Der Menschensohn und seine Sendung an die Menschheit," *Allgemeine Missions-Zeitschrift.* 20:149-178.

Kasdorf, Hans

1970 "Church Discipline: A Redemptive Approach," *Journal of Church and Society.* 6 (Fall 1970):40-61.

1974 "Conversion in Church Mission Perspective." A Study paper on the relationship between the church and the convert. (Xeroxed.)

Keeney, William

1973-74 "Salvation: Static or Dynamic?" MCC Peace Section (Elkhart, Ind.). (Xeroxed.)

Keysser, Christian

1929 *Eine Papuagemeinde.* Kassel: Bärenreiter-Verlag.

1949 *Gottes Weg ins Hubeland.* 2d ed. Neuendettelsau: Freimund-Verlag.

Kittel, Gerhard (ed.)

1964 *Theological Dictionary of the New Testament.* Vol. I. Translator and editor, Geoffrey W. Bromiley. Grand Rapids: Eerdmans.

Klaassen, Walter

1973 *Anabaptism: Neither Catholic nor Protestant.* Waterloo: Conrad Press.

Klassen, A. J. (ed.)

1970 *Consultation on Anabaptist Mennonite Theology.* Fresno: Council of Mennonite Seminaries.

Kohn, Hans

1965 *Nationalism: Its Meaning and History.* Revised edition. New York: Van Nostrand Reinhold Company.

Kraft, Charles H.

1973a "Toward a Christian Ethnotheology," in *God, Man and Church Growth.* A Festschrift in Honor of Donald Anderson McGavran. Edited by A. R. Tippett. Grand Rapids: Eerdmans, pp. 104-126.

1973b "Christianity and Culture." A manuscript produced

for distribution to students of Fuller Theological Seminary, Pasadena, Calif. (Xeroxed.)

Kroeber, Alfred Louis
1948 *Anthropology*. Race, Language, Culture, Psychology, Pre-History. New York: Harcourt, Brace and World, Inc.

Kroeker, Jakob
1949 *Der Römerbrief*. Kassel: Oncken Verlag.

Kuen, Alfred
1975 *Gemeindebau nach Gottes Bauplan*. Neuhausen-Stuttgart: Hänssler-Verlag.

Küng, Hans
1967 *The Church*. Translated by Ray and Rosaleen Ockenden. New York: Sheed and Ward.

Laubach, Fritz
1956 *Bekehrung und Wiedergeburt in biblischer Sicht*. Wuppertal: Verlag R. Brockhaus.

Legiehn, Hans
1954 *Unser Glaube ist der Sieg*. Ponta Grossa (Parana, Brazil): Editora Luz e Vida.

Leon, Jorge A.
1975 "Guilt Conversion and Modern Psychology," in *Let the Earth Hear His Voice*. Edited by J. D. Douglas. Minneapolis: World Wide Publications, pp. 1154-1160.

Littell, Franklin H.
1961 *A Tribute to Menno Simons*. Scottdale: Herald Press.
1972 *The Origins of Sectarian Protestantism*. Third Printing. New York: Macmillan.

Loewen, Jacob A.
1968 "The Indigenous Church and Resocialization," *Practical Anthropology*. 15:193-204.
1969 "Socialization and Conversion in the Ongoing Church," *Practical Anthropology*. 16:1-17.

Löffler, Paul
1967a "Conversion. Introduction," *The Ecumenical Review*. 19:349-351.

1967b "Conversion in an Ecumenical Context," *The Ecumenical Review.* 19:252-260.

1969 "The Christian Concept of 'Conversion to God' in Ecumenical and Missionary Perspective," *The Near East School of Theology Quarterly.* (January and April): 1-21.

Luther, Martin

1526 "The German Mass and Order of Service," in *Luther's Works.* American Edition. Vol. LIII: *Liturgy and Hymns.* Edited by Ulrich S. Leupold. Philadelphia: Fortress Press, 1965.

Luther, Ralf

1951 *Neutestamentliches Wörterbuch.* Thirteenth revised and enlarged edition. Hamburg: Furche-Verlag.

Luzbetak, Louis J.

1970 *The Church and Cultures.* Techny, Ill.: Divine Word.

Mark, Leslie E.

1975 "Cheap Grace?" *Christian Leader.* June 10:2-5.

Maslow, Abraham Harold

1964 *Religions, Values, and Peak Experiences.* Columbus: Ohio State University Press.

McGavran, Donald A.

1955a *The Bridges of God.* A Study in the Strategy of Missions. New York: Friendship Press.

1955b *How Churches Grow.* The New Frontiers in Mission. New York: Friendship Press.

1973 "The Mehra People Movement." In Pickett, et al. *Church Growth and Group Conversion.* 5th ed. South Pasadena: William Carey Library, pp. 71-83.

McQuilkin, J. Robertson

1973 *How Biblical Is the Church Growth Movement?* Chicago: Moody Press.

Mead, Margaret

1956 *New Lives for Old.* Cultural Transformation—Manus, 1928-1953. New York: William Morrow.

Meihuizen, H. W.

1970 "The Concept of Restitution in the Anabaptism of

North Western Europe." Translated by William Keeney. *Mennonite Quarterly Review*. 44:140-158.

Michel, Otto
1941 "Gottesherrschaft und Volkerwelt," *Evangelische Missionszeitschrift*. 2:225-233.

Mooneyham, W. Stanley
1976 *What Do You Say to a Hungry World?* Waco, Tex.: Word Books.

Newbigin, Lesslie
1969 *The Finality of Christ*. Richmond: John Knox Press.

Niebuhr, H. Richard
1963 *The Responsible Self*. An Essay in Christian Moral Philosophy. New York: Harper and Row.

Niles, D. T.
1962 *Upon the Earth*. The Mission of God and the Missionary Enterprise of the Churches. New York: McGraw Hill.

Nissiotis, Nikos A.
1967 "Conversion and the Church," *The Ecumenical Review*. 19:261-270.

Nock, A. D.
1972 *Conversion*. The Old and the New in Religion from Alexander the Great to Augustine of Hippo. London and New York: Oxford University Press.

Oliver, Dennis M. (ed.)
1975 "Church Growth Countdown," *Church Growth: Canada*. 2, No. 1:1

Olson, Bruce E.
1973 *For this Cross I'll Kill You*. Carol Stream, Ill.: Creation House.

Orr, J. Edwin
1973 *The Flaming Tongue*. The Impact of 20th Century Revivals. Chicago: Moody Press.

Ostermann, Eduard
1975 *Zukunft ohne Hoffnung?* Neuhausen-Stuttgart: Hänssler-Verlag.

Padilla, C. René (ed.)

> 1976 *The New Face of Evangelicalism.* An International Symposium on the Lausanne Covenant. Downers Grove: InterVarsity Press.

Peters, G. W.

> 1963 "The Meaning of Conversion," *Bibliotheca Sacra.* 120:234-242.

Pickett, J. Waskom

> 1933 *Christian Mass Movements in India.* Lucknow: Lucknow Publishing House, India.

> 1973 "The Gara Revival," in Pickett, et al. *Church Growth and Group Conversion.* 5th ed. South Pasadena: William Carey Library, pp. 21-35.

Pickett, J. Waskom; A. L. Warnshuis; G. H. Sing; and D. A. McGavren

> 1973 *Church Growth and Group Conversion.* 5th ed. (First Lucknow edition, 1936.) South Pasadena: William Carey Library.

Preuschen, Erwin

> 1910 *Vollständiges Griechisch-Deutsches Handwörterbuch zu den Schriften des Neuen Testaments und der übrigen urchristlichen Literatur.* Giessen: Verlag Alfred Töppelmann.

Raines, Robert A.

> 1961 *New Life in the Church.* New York: Harper and Row.

Ramseyer, Robert L.

> 1970 "The Revitalization Theory Applied to the Anabaptists," *Mennonite Quarterly Review.* 44:159-180.

Ray, Chandu

> 1973 "Fourth World and Asian Missionaries," *Church Growth Bulletin.* 6:342-343.

Richardson, Don

> 1974 *Peace Child.* Glendale: Regal Books.

Rienecker, Fritz

> 1967 *Lexikon zur Bibel.* 6th ed. Wuppertal: Verlag R. Brockhaus.

Salzman, Leon

   1966 "Types of Religious Conversion," *Pastoral Psychology*.
        17:8-20.

Sanders, J. Oswald.

   1974 *The Holy Spirit and His Gifts*. Ninth Printing. Grand
        Rapids: Zondervan.

Schärer, Hans

   1944 *Die Begründung der Mission in der katholischen und
        evangelischen Missionswissenschaft*. Theologische
        Studien Heft 16. Edited by Karl Barth. Zollikon-
        Zürich: Evangelischer Verlag.

Scheffbuch, Winrich

   1973 *Christen unter Hammer und Sichel*. 3d ed. Wuppertal:
        R. Brockhaus Verlag.

Schlatter, Adolf

   1948 *Der Brief an die Römer*. Stuttgart: Calwer Verlag.

Schmitz, Richard, and Wilhelm Wöhrle

   1962 *Das Herrnmahl*. Witten (Ruhr): Bundes-Verlag.

Shank, David A.

   1976 "Towards an Understanding of Christian Conversion."
        Mission-Focus Magazine, Vol. 5, No. 2 (November
        1976): 1-7.

Sharpe, Eric

   1969 "The Problem of Conversion in Recent Missionary
        Thought." *Evangelical Quarterly* XL1, 4:221-231.

Simons, Menno

   1956 *The Complete Writings of Menno Simons*. Translated
        from the Dutch by Leonard Verduin and edited by
        John C. Wenger. Scottdale: Herald Press.

Stott, John R. W.

   1975 *Christian Mission in the Modern World*. Downers
        Grove: InterVarsity Press.

   1976 "Response to Bishop Mortimer Arias," *International
        Review of Mission*. 65:30-34.

Strachan, R. Kenneth

   1968 *The Inescapable Calling*. Grand Rapids: Eerdmans.

Taylor, A. E.

    1953 *Socrates: The Man and His Thought.* Garden City: Garden City Anchor Book.

Taylor, John V.

    1965 *Du findest mich wenn du den Stein aufhebst.* Translated from *The Primal Vision* (SCM Press, London, 1963) by Christoph and Gertrud Hahn. München: Christian Kaiser Verlag.

Thomas, W. H. Griffith.

    1976 *St. Paul's Epistle to the Romans.* Eleventh Printing. Grand Rapids: Eerdmans.

Tippett, Alan R.

    1971 *People Movements in Southern Polynesia.* A Study in Church Growth. Chicago: Moody Press.

    1972 "Possessing the Philosophy of Animism to Christ," in *Crucial Issues in Missions Tomorrow.* Edited by Donald A. McGavran. Chicago: Moody Press, pp. 125-144.

    1973 *Verdict Theology in Missionary Theory.* South Pasadena: William Carey Library.

    1974 "Extension to the Cross-Cultural Conversion Model." Research in Progress Pamphlet #13. Fuller Theological Seminary, Pasadena.

Toews, John E.

    1975 "The Church . . . Discerning Brotherhood, Not Preacherhood." *Christian Leader,* August 5:4-6.

Trueblood, Elton

    1961 *The Company of the Committed.* New York: Harper & Row.

    1972 *The Validity of the Christian Mission.* New York: Harper & Row.

Vicedom, Georg

    1960 *Missio Dei.* 2d ed. München: Christian Kaiser Verlag.

    1962 "An Example of Group Conversion," *Practical Anthropology* (now issued as *Missiology*). 9:123-128.

    1969 *Mission in einer Zeit der Revolution.* Wuppertal: Theologischer Verlag R. Brockhaus.

Vine, W. E.

    1948a *Expository Dictionary of New Testament Words*. Vol. II. London: Oliphants, Ltd.

    1948b *Expository Dictionary of New Testament Words*. Vol IV. London: Oliphants, Ltd.

Von Bismark, Klaus

    1957 "The Christian Vocabulary: An Obstacle to Communication?" *The Ecumenical Review*. 10:1-15.

Wagner, C. Peter

    1972 *Church/Mission Tensions*. Chicago: Moody Press, pp. 215-222.

Wallace, Anthony F. C.

    1956 "Revitalization Movements," *American Anthropologist*. 58:264-281.

    1970 *Culture and Personality*. New York: Random House Publishers.

Ward, Barbara.

    1962 *The Rich Nations and the Poor Nations*. New York: W. W. Norton and Co., Inc.

    1964 *Towards a World of Plenty?* Toronto: University of Toronto Press.

    1966 *Spaceship Earth*. New York: Columbia University Press.

Warneck, Gustav

    1874 "Der Missionsbefehl als Missionsinstruction," *Allgemeine Missionszeitschrift*. 1:41-49; 89-92; 137-151; 185-194; 233-239; 281-290; 277-292.

    1902 *Evangelische Missionslehre*, Bd. III, 1: *Der Betrieb der Sendung*. 2d ed. Gotha: Perthes, pp. 243-286.

Warnshuis, A. L.

    1973 "Group Conversion," in Pickett, et al., *Church Growth and Group Conversion*. 5th ed. South Pasadena: William Carey Library, pp. 8-20.

Wiens, Delbert

    1965 *New Wineskins for Old Wine*. Hillsboro, Kan.: Mennonite Brethren Publishing House.

Williams, George H.

    1975 *The Radical Reformation*. Third Printing. Philadelphia: Westminster Press.

Williamson, Lowell and Naomi

    1969 "A Sorcerer Tells His Story," *The Missionary Standard*. May, pp. 3-5.

Winter, Ralph D.

    1970 *The 25 Unbelievable Years 1945-1969*. South Pasadena: William Carey Library.

    1972 "Quality or Quantity?" in *Crucial Issues in Missions Tomorrow*. Edited by Donald A. McGavran. Chicago: Moody Press, pp. 175-187.

Wirt, Sherwood Eliot

    1968 *The Social Conscience of the Evangelical*. New York: Harper and Row.

Wonderly, William L.

    1968 *Bible Translations for Popular Use*. London: United Bible Societies.

Worship Hymnal

    1971 Hillsboro, Kan.: Mennonite Brethren Publishing House.

Wright, G. Ernest

    1969 *God Who Acts*. Biblical Theology as Recital. London: SCM Press, Ltd.

Yoder, John Howard

    1972 *The Original Revolution*. Scottdale, Pa.: Herald Press.

Scripture Reference Index

General Index

Hans Kasdorf currently heads the Department of World Mission and directs the Church Mission Institute at Mennonite Brethren Biblical Seminary, Fresno, California.

He has written many mission-related articles for academic journals, has contributed to numerous books, and has authored *Gemeindewachstum als missionarisches Ziel* (1976). He is preparing a German adaptation of *Christian Conversion in Context* for publication by Verlag der Liebenzeller Mission (1981). A member of the Board of Mission and Services of the Mennonite Brethren Church, Kasdorf is frequently called on to speak at mission conferences and seminars in North America, Latin America, and Europe.

The youngest in a family of nine children, Hans Kasdorf was born in Slawgorod, Siberia, in 1928. As a young child he moved with his family and other Mennonite families to the interior of southern Brazil.

Though much of his adult life has been devoted to academic endeavors, his childhood and youth were marked by a lack of educational opportunities. Since his family was poor and needed his help to make a living, young Hans dropped out of school after grade two. He did not own his first book until age nineteen.

In the course of a dynamic renewal movement, the author experienced personally at age eighteen what he talks about in this book—Christian conversion. He was subsequently baptized and became an active member of the believers' church.

With a strong desire for education and a sense of call to Christian service, Kasdorf moved to Canada where he received seven years of Bible training. Eventually he completed high school and took university courses by correspondence. He has also done graduate work at the University of Oregon, Mennonite Brethren Biblical Seminary in Fresno, California, and the School of World Mission at Fuller Theological Seminary in Pasadena, where he earned degrees in modern languages and literature, evangelism and missions, historical theology, and missiology.

The author is married to Frieda Reimer, formerly of Yarrow, British Columbia. The Kasdorfs have three children, including a married daughter, and are members of the Butler Avenue Mennonite Brethren Church in Fresno.